KERRY R TYACK

NEW ZEALAND BEERS

A TASTING GUIDE

To my sons Oliver and Findlay. May they grow to appreciate well-made beer, respect its place in their lives, and enjoy discovering the provenance and rituals associated with one of history's greatest inventions.

PENGUIN BOOKS
Published by the Penguin Group
Penguin Group (NZ), cnr Airborne and Rosedale Roads, Albany,
Auckland 1310, New Zealand (a division of Pearson New Zealand Ltd)
Penguin Group (USA) Inc., 375 Hudson Street,
New York, New York 10014, USA
Penguin Group (Canada), 10 Alcorn Avenue, Toronto,
Ontario, Canada M4V 3B2 (a division of Pearson Penguin Canada Inc.)
Penguin Books Ltd, 80 Strand, London, WC2R 0RL, England
Penguin Ireland, 25 St Stephen's Green,
Dublin 2, Ireland (a division of Penguin Books Ltd)
Penguin Group (Australia), 250 Camberwell Road, Camberwell,
Victoria 3124, Australia (a division of Pearson Australia Group Pty Ltd)
Penguin Books India Pvt Ltd, 11, Community Centre,
Panchsheel Park, New Delhi - 110 017, India
Penguin Books (South Africa) (Pty) Ltd, 24 Sturdee Avenue,
Rosebank, Johannesburg 2196, South Africa

Penguin Books Ltd, Registered Offices: 80 Strand, London, WC2R 0RL, England

This edition published by Penguin Group (NZ), 2005
10 9 8 7 6 5 4 3 2 1

Packaged for Penguin by Renée Lang, Renaissance Publishing
Cover design: Gina Hochstein
Text design: Alison Dench
Printed in Australia by McPherson's Printing Group

ISBN 0 14 302029 3

A catalogue record for this book is available
from the National Library of New Zealand.

www.penguin.co.nz

Thanks to The HomeStore, Newmarket, Auckland, for providing the pilsner glass for the cover shot

CONTENTS

ACKNOWLEDGEMENTS

WITH THE EXCEPTION OF the tasting notes, which are all my own, the information in this book is gathered from brewers, large and small, around the country. My thanks to those who gave freely of their time, their product and their experience to assist me in making this guide as up to date as possible.

Unfortunately, not every brewery wanted to be mentioned, especially one or two who found my previous descriptions of their beer unpalatable. I regret their decision as chances are their beers have improved since my last sampling. My advice is to visit them anyway and make your own assessment of their products. Your feedback will no doubt be of great value.

Also, not every beer from every brewery was tasted. Some beers are seasonal and were not available at the time of my visit; others were in the process of being brewed; and others were only available from the brewery door in small quantities.

However, it seems to me that if you get to try even a small proportion of the beers mentioned here, your understanding and appreciation of New Zealand beer will have grown enormously.

PREFACE

BEER CONTINUES TO PLAY a significant role in shaping New Zealand society. It remains a key element in much of our conviviality and entertainment; it is almost always present at social gatherings involving celebration and commemoration. Brewing employs thousands of people and contributes substantially to the nation's economy. The bigger breweries, as well as touting their products, continue to support community activities, sponsoring sport and cultural endeavour, and have been both courted and criticised for their efforts.

Craft brews are increasingly visible and the range of products available to the Kiwi beer drinker continues to grow.

Among the beers available in New Zealand we have brands that will last only until someone actually tastes them, and beers that have repeatedly won the highest international accolades. We have quaffers and speciality beers; we have high-strength and low-strength beers; we have hand-made and mass-produced beers. This guide celebrates the diversity of the New Zealand beer industry and wishes it long life!

INTRODUCTION

IT IS AN UNDENIABLE part of beer's appeal that we are constantly being challenged by innovative renditions of familiar recipes, as well as exposed to entirely new brews. In the introduction to the 2002 edition of this guide, I noted that our brewing environment had changed. It is fair to say that it has altered even more in the intervening three years and that this 'state of constant adjustment' is likely to be permanent. Breweries close, brewers change camps, new products are launched and energetic newcomers establish new production companies, all making it very difficult to ensure a guide like this one remains up to date!

I am happy to report that since 2002 a few new breweries have opened. Sadly, more have closed. Some familiar names in the industry are no longer around, having moved on to other pursuits, while some of my favourite brands are no longer being produced.

While I am always saddened by the news of a brewery closure, I take heart from the fact that those that remain, by and large, have improved the quality of their beers. In addition, I am buoyed by the positive influence the sale of beer in supermarkets has had on the range of beer styles now within easy reach of the average beer drinker. There are literally hundreds of interesting brands on supermarket and liquor shop shelves. But, while the Kiwi beer consumer may well be spoilt for choice, it is still not smooth sailing for our own craft brewing industry. As in previous editions, most of the beers reviewed in this guide come from small craft breweries. Unfortunately, there are very few brewers in this country who can easily marry the truly commercial approach to brewing with the demands of producing limited quantities of high-quality craft brews. Those producers who have no packaged product to sell but rather rely on brewery door sales or bulk beer deliveries are facing tough competition from the mass producers.

Some smaller producers have taken up the challenge and are looking to invest in bottling plant in order to gain retail shelf space for their products and thereby greater consumer recognition. But this is a major investment that needs to be well considered and carefully planned and, sadly, it remains outside the resources of many small companies.

Chris O'Leary from Limburg Brewing Company, Richard Emerson from Emerson's, Alan Absalom from Miner's, John Duncan from Founders, Dick Fife from Dux de Lux and John Harrington from Harrington's in Christchurch are among those brewers who successfully bridge the gap between commercial and craft brewer.

Brewers such as Keith Galbraith of Galbraith, Barry Newman of Shakespeare Tavern & Brewery, Kieran Meyer from The Cock & Bull and the guys from the Loaded Hog all do an excellent job of getting their beers in front of customers in their respective venues. Others, such as Geoff Logan and Gerry Maude from Sunshine Brewing Company, continue to make the most of their niche.

Still other brewers simply do not want to enter the world of high-volume consumables and are happy enough to service their local, and loyal customer base. They see no need to gear up to compete with major companies. Good on them, I say. Brewing is for many a labour of love, an opportunity to produce something they have a passion for. Those who wish to simply pursue their dream within their own communities should be supported.

At the end of the day most of the beer consumed in New Zealand is brewed by either DB Breweries or Lion Breweries — the two big guys — with help from some moderately sized regional cooperatives.

While my own palate is perhaps more regularly excited by the less commercial beers on offer, I am not prepared to denigrate the big breweries for promoting their brews. To do so is to inherently accuse those who enjoy their products of having no taste or appreciation of beer styles other than mainstream.

This attitude would also fail to recognise that on occasion the big breweries or their subsidiaries are capable of producing a much better than average beer. Mac's, for example, has one or two products that are easily a class above the ordinary Kiwi brown beer. Monteith's is capable of brewing some exceptional seasonal beers and Speight's has done a good job at exploring what is possible to achieve in a big brewery environment with the development of their craft beer range.

There is still considerable angst in New Zealand brewing circles that seems to derive from a deeply entrenched 'them and us' attitude. It is difficult to understand at times why smaller breweries should fear the bigger guys or why indeed the major companies should see the smaller producers as any kind of threat. The numbers do not stack up in either case.

The true beer lover should, to my mind, acknowledge that bigger producers selling commercial brews create an advantage for all brewers by keeping beer in the forefront of the consumer's mind, this at a time when demands on disposable income from all manner of competing beverage products are increasing.

For their part the major producers should acknowledge that craft brewers in New Zealand are helping to expand the overall market. The smaller producers contribute plenty in terms of keeping interest in beer alive and niche breweries are instrumental in exposing the consumer to a huge range of tastes, flavours and styles. New Zealand's craft brewers are successfully pushing boundaries and creating news where ordinary stock brands of beer tend to be cynically ignored. There is a place for all kinds of beer in New Zealand and all size and manner of producer.

This, the third edition of the beer guide, is my way of assisting beer lovers and those just beginning their journey of beer discovery to celebrate diversity, cultivate variety and energetically explore the art of the possible. When we accept that there is a place for all kinds of beer, the New Zealand beer consumer will be better off than ever before and visitors to this country will become even more aware of just how good our brewers have become.

FROM GRAIN TO BREW ————

THE MAKING OF BEER IS, on one level, a comparatively simple process. No matter how different or innovative a beer is, the process used to make it will have followed a pattern common to almost every brewer in the world. In fact, the process of transforming a few key ingredients into beer can be managed by any competent home brewer, provided certain basic conditions are met.

On another level, brewing is an enormously complex task, more complicated in fact than making wine for example. On the one hand, the big commercial breweries aiming to produce vast quantities of beer that tastes exactly the same brew after brew are faced with the challenge of consistency. On the other hand, small craft brewers seeking that stylistically perfect beer have the challenge of definition to deal with, in addition to the search for appropriate ingredients, the maintenance of brewery hygiene and the management of issues of batch differentiation.

What can safely be said is that all beer is the result of a fermentation process and all beer uses, to a varying degree, the same four key ingredients, combined according to variations on the same recipe. Those ingredients are: grain, most often barley; fresh, clean, pure water; hops to taste; and yeast. Of course, the resulting beers will vary widely, depending on whether the beer is batch brewed or the result of continuous fermentation; whether it is the product of a very large or a very small brewery; whether any additives have been used, etc. Some of these variables may be of minor importance only while others can have a significant impact. However, essentially, making beer is a straightforward task.

> **BEER QUOTES** 'Wine is more vulnerable to the mercies of soil and weather, but beer is the more complicated to make.' Michael Jackson, *Michael Jackson's Pocket Beer Book*

THE BEER-MAKING PROCESS

STEP 1 MALTING

First, cereal grains are malted. During this process the grain is soaked with water and allowed to begin germinating, then dried under controlled conditions. Some very good beer is made with wheat, maize or rice, but barley is the easiest grain to malt and so it has, over time, become the favoured grain used in the vast majority of beers. Today, the malting process takes place at specialised malting factories and the malted barley is delivered to the brewer in bulk form.

STEP 2 MASHING

Once at the brewery, the malted grain is milled and mixed with hot water in the mash tun (a large cask). It is heated to boiling point to extract natural enzymes and the soluble sugars of the malt. During this process the starch from the malt is converted to fermentable sugars.

STEP 3 BOILING

The slurry (consisting of liquid and the malt husks) that results from the mashing process is put in a filtration vessel called a 'lauter'. Here the dissolved sugars, in the form of a liquid called 'wort' (pronounced 'wurt'), are separated from the husks and are transferred to a kettle and boiled to develop colour and flavour.

Hops can be added now or later in the process. If the hops are added at this stage, the boiling process sees the bitter compounds extracted from the hops.

Some brewers still use the hop flower head, while others use hops that have been processed into pellet form. Early forms of beer were made without hops, using other aromatics and flavouring additives, like cinnamon and cardamom, instead. It was not until about the 13th century that Bavarian and German monks discovered that the addition of hops, the bitter herb grown in monastery gardens, helped to preserve and flavour the beer. Nowadays, it is rare for a beer to be made without hops.

The boiling wort is stirred by means of a whirlpool that also serves to clarify the liquid by centrifugal force.

STEP 4 FERMENTATION

Next, the brew is cooled to 10–15°C and put into the fermenter, where yeast is added. The living yeast converts sugars to alcohol and carbon dioxide.

Beer is categorised into two major styles, lagers and ales, according to the type of yeast used in the fermentation process. Traditionally, bottom or 'lager' yeast is used for beers that are fermented at lower temperatures and for longer periods, e.g. lager, pilsener, marzen and bock. Ales and other older styles are usually brewed at a higher temperature using top yeasts that give more fruity beers with a flavour more heavily influenced by the fermentation process.

STEP 5 MATURATION AND PACKAGING

At this point the 'green beer' is usually placed in containers to mature at below 0°C. The maturation process can last for anything from a few days to a few months. (Some craft brewers have reverted to the old style where the beer is put straight into bottles and allowed to mature there.) Finally, the 'bright' beer is taken from its maturation containers and clarified by means of settling and filtration, and then packaged.

MATCHING FOOD AND BEER———

THE CONCEPT IS SIMPLE: choosing the right beer to accompany the right food will enhance your enjoyment of both. While mixing haute cuisine with the much-loved brown stuff may be a new idea to the average Kiwi, the notion of serving beer with food is neither new nor peculiar. Brewhouses, cafés and wayside inns have been around for centuries and they have always involved the serving of food. Wherever beer is served in Europe you see counter lunches, pies, ploughman's lunches, biersticks, beer batter, beer bread, pizza, and so on. You only have to look at paintings by Bruegel and other European Masters to see how often a tankard of ale is set down beside the roast game or a platter of bread and cheese. Basic, hearty fare was the order of the day and while today the food options are much broader the exploration of combinations remains valid. Recognition of this comes in the ever-expanding library of books on beer and food from authors all around the world.

Beer drinkers' palates are changing and developing, becoming more sensitive as tasters become more knowledgeable. In general, we are taking more time to sample and savour different brands, to appreciate style and aroma, to distinguish between flavours and to appreciate the craftsmanship that provides strong, individual characteristics in each beer. A logical step in this process is the restoration of beer as a valid option when looking for a beverage to accompany and enhance meals.

When matching beer with food there are some important things to keep in mind. The process can be as complex, tantalising, varied and exciting as that of matching wine and food. As with wine matching, no one beer will combine with all foods in a way that satisfies

> **BEER QUOTES** 'Good food and good beer form, in every sense of the word, a perfect marriage.'
> Peter La France, *Cooking and Eating with Beer*

everyone's palate. Most beers go with most food, but finding a superb beer/food match is more of a challenge. The quest is for synergy — neither the beer nor the food should overwhelm the other. Rather, they should be better in combination than they are apart.

Of course, matching beer and food is very much a subjective process, but here are some guidelines that will assist those thinking of giving it a go.

THINK REGIONAL
It is likely that a beer style from a particular region will combine best with the cuisine style of the same region. There is good reason for this. Boutique brewers have been the rule as opposed to the exception around the world, so beer — until the advent of modern transportation — has always had a strong regional connection. For centuries beer was made in small batches by home and village brewers, using local ingredients and was subject to local brewing conditions. Consequently, the flavour of these beers reflected the local *terroir*, to borrow a hip winemaking term. It is logical, therefore, to look first at the range of local ingredients that might influence the cuisine to find what scope there is for finding that ideal beer/food combination.

THINK STYLE
All styles of beer have completely individual textures, aromas and flavours. To make an appropriate beer/food choice, therefore, it is important to educate yourself. Learn to distinguish a lager from a pilsner (pilsener, pils), a Guinness from a stout. Find out more about brewing and the processes that contribute to the taste profiles. Build up a vocabulary of appropriate terms so that when discussing beer you are able to share your thoughts about the flavours you pick up.

THINK AROMA
Aroma is very important because our sense of smell is so closely tied to our sense of taste. Paying attention to a beer's aroma is the first step in the tasting process. Take time to lift the glass to your nose and form an opinion as to what fragrances you can identify. Common characteristics are the flowery and herbal nose of a well-brewed lager and the maltiness of a Bavarian-style beer. Often ales leave an impression of fruitiness.

THINK FLAVOUR AND TEXTURE
Flavour, naturally, is the most important characteristic. Considering the influence of each ingredient and the particular beer style on the final product will definitely aid in the

food-matching process. Begin with a generous mouthful and swirl it around so that it covers all the palate before swallowing. The 'body' of a beer, as with wine, ranges from thin to full with the same general matching principles. The perceived thickness of a beer comes from its grain-to-water ratio. Carbonation should also be considered because an overly effervescent beer hampers the ability of the palate to taste. Look for a smooth, elegant, complex finish and note whether it quickly disappears or lingers a little. See the Flavour Wheel opposite for hints on how to describe a beer's flavour.

MAKE YOUR MATCH

When matching beer with food the choices are as complex as you want them to be, but the end result can be simply wonderful.

When considering a menu think about dishes that emphasise wholesome ingredients in keeping with the natural ingredients and processing involved in the making of beer. Try to achieve a high degree of compatibility between the beer and the menu in terms of texture, flavour and balance. The chemistry of the mouth is changed by food and one's appreciation of the beer changes accordingly. The main thing is to keep it simple — match like with like.

The less sweet the food, the drier the beer should be. Pair a delicate shellfish dish with a pale ale or mild lager, both of which are made using light and subtle ingredients. If you increase the seasoning or choose more strongly flavoured ingredients, the beer should also be more intense, perhaps an amber ale or dark lager. Darker beers — porters and stouts — all beautifully balance red meats in rich sauces and gravies. They also go well with savoury spiced meats like corned beef or the traditional roast.

Beer is a perfect foil for ethnic, especially spicy, cuisine. Water only spreads the chilli around; a pilsener, light amber or mild wheat beer will soothe the palate and refresh the mouth. The higher the alcohol content, the more soothing the beer will be.

Many beers make excellent aperitifs as the bitterness produced by the hops stimulates the appetite by increasing the production of gastric juices.

THINK PRESENTATION

Get in the habit of presenting a beer at its best. The temperature generally should be 6–8°C, although typically in New Zealand beer is drunk at around 3–4°C. Serve a good-quality beer in a good-quality glass. While appearance is not strictly important when matching a beer with food, it is part of the enjoyment to see the appropriate colour, clarity and head for the beer style. The glass should be clear and cleaned of any soap residue.

THE FLAVOUR WHEEL

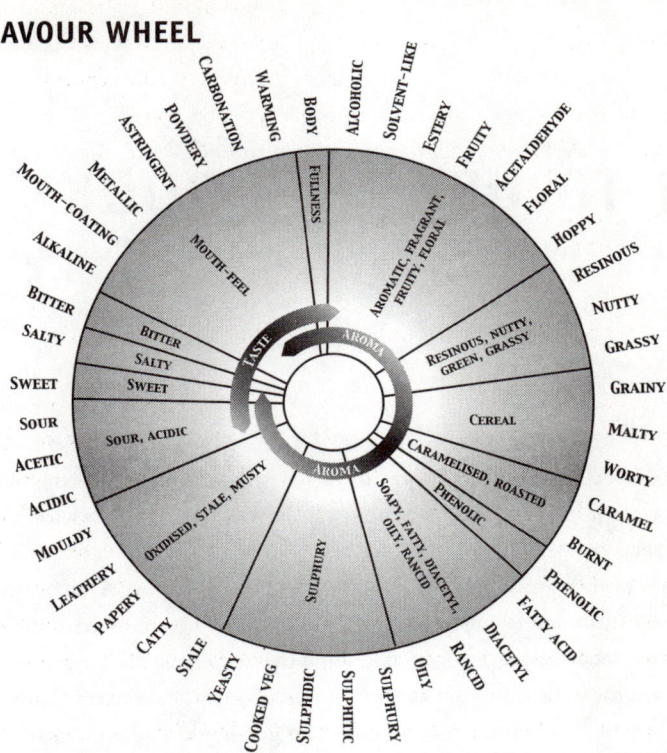

The flavour wheel is a simple but effective tool used by brewers to nominate the character of a beer. It can be used to identify aroma, mouth-feel and taste — all of which contribute to flavour. The descriptors on the wheel are common traits you can expect to find in beer.

The wheel works like a clock. When sampling a beer begin with the aroma. The aroma section of the flavour wheel begins at 12 o'clock, in the top right-hand section. Follow the wheel around in a clockwise direction to decide which term best describes the aroma. If, for example, it reminds you of newly cut grass you can go to the second section, where you can decide whether your beer is resinous, nutty or grassy. Then move on to taste. For example, if the beer has a sour taste go to the section at 9 o'clock and decide whether it is sour, acetic or acidic, somewhere in between or a combination of all sorts of sour.

One word of caution: clearly some of the descriptors on the flavour wheel are negative. Nobody enjoys a 'rancid' beer, for example. But it shouldn't be assumed that words such as 'burnt' are always negative — many dark beers have a burnt-toast character that is acceptable as part of the beer's style.

These descriptors are not intended to provide an exhaustive list. There are many, many other adjectives that can be used to describe a beer's flavour. Treat these as a guide only.

HOW TO USE THIS BOOK ⸺

THIS BOOK IS INTENDED as a reference point for those looking for information on beers produced in New Zealand, where they are made and who makes them. My suggestion would be to place it in the glovebox of your car, in your suitcase or briefcase, backpack or handbag. In this way, wherever your travels take you, you can consult the guide to find out what breweries beer treasures you can expect to find in the region. As in previous editions, this guide also features an extensive tasting list of imported beers (see pages 153–180).

The contact details are as accurate as I could make them at the time of going to print. But be prepared for some deviation as phone numbers change, breweries move and brands are born or deleted. The list of breweries is set out geographically from north to south and includes all the breweries I could identify. In addition, the guide provides a list of the beers available at the various breweries and a personal view of the impression they left on me on the day I tried them. Those beers featuring a 'Top Brew' icon particularly appealed; some are consistent favourites, others are newer discoveries. Of course, my opinion is only something to get you started. You must try them for yourself and form your own judgements.

The tasting notes are given in the order I tasted them. I formed my opinions from a single tasting from a single batch. For many brewers change is part and parcel of the process of brewing: on the day you visit you may form a completely different view and that's exactly how it should be. While I am not actively seeking feedback , should you wish to share your views of the beers you try, feel free to write to me (kerryt@wave.co.nz).

Lastly, when you visit those breweries that are open to the public, seek out the brewer and offer him or her feedback and encouragement. Ask your questions, show your interest. It's what many of them thrive on and need to keep them positive about the way they go about their craft.

NORTH ISLAND BREWERIES —

Twin Pines

Hokianga Breweries ●

● Sawmill

Pilot Bay Brewing ● ● Waiheke Island Brewery

Bean Rock
The Loaded Hog
Shakespeare
Lion
Galbraith
Trident
Waitemata Brewery
Steam
Independent

Sunshine ●

● White Cliffs

Roosters ● Mates
Limburg

Waituna ●

Shamrock ● ● Tui

Tuatara ●

Martinborough Beer & Ales
Island Bay Brewing ● ● Wellington Brewing

TWIN PINES RESTAURANT AND BAR

ADDRESS
Puketona Road,
RD 1, Paihia

PHONE
(09) 402 7195

FAX
(09) 402 7193

BREWER
Steven Nicholls

OPEN
Mon–Sun 12 noon–
1 am (summer)
Mon–Sun 3 pm–
1 am (winter)

Twin Pines Steak & Ale House is owned by the Nicholls family. It is one of the few old hotel restaurant and bar businesses still operating up north and is located in a wonderful 120-year-old building in one of New Zealand's busiest tourist districts. It is also fortunate enough to have full brewing facilities. Owner Steven Nicholls oversees all the brewing and when need arises, brings in a bit of expertise from breweries nearby, including the guys from Hokianga Breweries. Two beers are made on site: a dark ale and a more mainstream lager. There is the capacity to brew up to 10,000 litres at any time but they usually brew just enough to cater for the customers at their restaurant and bar. It is Steve's dream that in the not-too-distant future there will be the resources and demand to bottle his fine product for general sale.

BREWHOUSE LAGER

ALCOHOL
4% abv

STYLE
Golden Lager

A standard golden-brown lager made for easy drinking, this beer has a strong aroma of wet hay and grapefruit. It is light in weight with a slightly thin mouth-feel that accentuates the citrus fruit character. There is plenty of hop evident in the taste — perhaps a more judicious use of this strong ingredient would improve the overall balance of the brew. This is a much-improved version on previous tastings, but whatever food you choose to accompany it should have a sweetish flavour to add contrast and balance. Alternatively, you could choose something deep fried that will benefit from the cut-through of the beer. Fish and chips would be a good place to start your experimenting.

BREWHOUSE DARK

ALCOHOL
4% abv

STYLE
Dark Lager

A true, deep, dark brown in colour, Brewhouse Dark has a strong aroma of Marmite, with a lick of Christmas cake fruit thrown in for good measure. The texture is reasonably thin and there is little aftertaste. You will pick up strong burnt-toast and coffee flavours; with the brew I tried still missing the benefit of a little malt sweetness.

The intensity of flavour is certainly admirable but there needs to be a more creamy texture to put the flavours into perspective and to carry them to the finish. Like the lager, this beer is definitely on the improve and is better when sampled with food. Traditional sausages served with caramelised onions and fries is my pick for a summer main course, or perhaps steak and kidney pie in cooler months.

HOKIANGA BREWERIES

ADDRESS
SH 12, Waimamaku, Kaikohe

PHONE/FAX
(09) 405 8681

BREWER
Innes Carrad

OPEN
Daily 10 am–5 pm

Hokianga Breweries, in the far north of the North Island, is the pride and pleasure of Innes Carrad and his family. Innes, a keen home brewer, decided his beer was good enough to be shared with the locals and tourists who called in to the small family café on the Hokianga Harbour. He bought the historic butcher's shop next door and created Hokianga Breweries. The staple brew is Coachmans Lager, but Innes brews a dark beer as well — although he does cause some confusion by using the same label ('Coachmans Ale') on both! For special occasions he puts down an Old Ale. Only New Zealand hops are used and the brews are dry hopped. No chemicals or cane sugar are added and the beers are unfiltered. Over the years a honing of brewing skills and the use of better quality ingredients have resulted in a dramatic improvement in Innes' beers and now he has punters coming from near and far for their unique taste of the north.

In the future Innes hopes to have his beers more widely available but at the moment they can be purchased only at the brewery, to enjoy with a light meal in the café or to take home in 745-millilitre bottles or 2-litre PETs.

COACHMANS LAGER

ALCOHOL
4% abv

STYLE
Pale Lager

Pale straw in colour with a slight green hue, this lager has a distinct but moderate hop aroma — not too strident, not too tame. The overall result is a pleasant enough, balanced brew. It is clean and crisp, with reasonably subtle flavours and a good, lingering bitterness. A favourite with the regulars, especially during the summer months, it is uncomplicated and, as with many lagers, best enjoyed with simple food such as open sandwiches or perhaps a cold platter of continental sausage (e.g. salami, bratwurst), pickled onions, gherkins and a tasty cheddar.

BLACK SHADOW 2000

This dark brown beer has an easily distinguishable hop aroma that is derived from the Hallertau hops used in its production, but you will also find plenty of malt and fruit character in the pleasant bouquet. The texture is crisp and clean and the flavour very malt driven, with oodles of fruitiness to balance a double dose of hops. It has good mouth-feel and plenty of length to satisfy those who enjoy the darker styles. Choose a mixed grill from the menu for a good match.

ALCOHOL
4% abv

STYLE
Dark Lager

SAWMILL BREWERY

A very new brewery situated on the east coast, about one and a half hours' drive north of Auckland, the Sawmill Brewery has the capacity to batch brew around 1200 litres at a time. Currently two variants are made — Bohemian Lager and Dopplebock. However, there are plans to expand this to a range of five or six. The beers are made using microfiltered rainwater and are available only from the café associated with the brewery.

Unfortunately no beer was available for tasting at the time of writing.

ADDRESS
142 Pakiri Road,
Leigh, Warkworth

PHONE
(09) 422 6555

MOBILE
0274 781 832

EMAIL
enquiry@eei.co.nz

WEBSITE
www.sawmillcafe.co.nz

BREWER
Peter Freckleton

OPEN
Daily 10 am–late
(summer)
See website for
winter opening
hours

PILOT BAY BREWING

Named after the area in the Bay of Plenty where the brewery was originally established, Pilot Bay beer (now brewed in Kumeu, near Auckland) is made the traditional way: slowly, carefully and using only malted barley, hops, yeast and water. The brewing team is proud of the fact that no chemicals, preservatives or sugars are added and Pilot Bay beer is allowed to mature for at least a month before packaging.

Pilot Bay beer is available from the cellar door at Riverhead Estate winery, north-west of Auckland, and from selected liquor merchants, restaurants, bars and clubs throughout New Zealand. Visitors are welcome at Riverhead Estate's restaurant, Glennies, to taste the beer and the range of fruit wine that is also made on site. Bookings are essential for tastings.

ADDRESS
1171 Coatesville/
Riverhead Highway
(SH28), Kumeu,
Auckland

PHONE
(09) 412 5555

FAX
(09) 412 7755

EMAIL
pilotbay@riverhead-estate.co.nz

WEBSITE
www.pilotbaybeer.co.nz

BREWER
Alan Lawes

OPEN
Mon–Sat 9 am–
4.30 pm

PILOT BAY LAGER

Beer writer Michael Jackson liked this beer when he visited New Zealand in 1997 and awarded it his Gold Medal. Pale gold in colour, it has a mild fruity aroma and a smooth, crisp texture in the style of European lager. The mouth-feel is light and the flavour characterised by slightly malt caramel aftertaste. It's pleasant drinking, although while there is a hint of hop bitterness on the back palate, a bit more length would cement its appeal. A good quaffing lager, sure to be a popular choice served well chilled on a hot day. It is a good match with spicy food — perhaps Cajun fish from the barbecue.

ALCOHOL
4% abv

STYLE
European-style
Lager

SCOTTISH WEE HEAVY

Originally brewed to celebrate events associated with a local Highland Games Society, this beer is now well entrenched as a Pilot Bay innovation. Brewed with Scottish malted barley to a traditional recipe, it is best served at around 8°C when its full flavour will be at its best.

ALCOHOL
5% abv

STYLE
A Wee Heavy

It is a medium brown colour with a slight red tinge. The aroma is of caramel and cold coffee with some fruitiness evident as well. The texture is smooth on the front with a slight graininess on the sides and back of the palate. It is full and flavourful with plenty of malt sweetness, some caramel and the merest hint of hop flavour towards the back of the palate. This is my pick of the Pilot Bay brews, more complex and challenging than the others. It's a good food beer, worth the effort of preparing something special — a decent, rich rabbit casserole with lots of root vegetables for me.

MANUKA HONEY BEER

Surprise, surprise, this one's honey coloured — medium straw with a touch of gold. A honey sweetness comes through in the aroma, the texture is creamy and the mouth-feel light. In flavour terms this beer is very mild with a light hand being used to add the native manuka honey, which imparts a subtle rather than dominating quality. This beer will appeal to the sweet tooth and be a welcome refresher served well chilled in the summer months. Try it with sweet and sour pork from your favourite Chinese food outlet.

ALCOHOL
4.8% abv

STYLE
Honey-infused Lager

WAIHEKE ISLAND BREWERY

The Waiheke Island Brewery was originally built in Tauranga and operated by McCashin's. The 1200-litre plant was brought to the island in 1997 and rolled out its first keg in January 1998. Since then its beers have gained wide distribution around the island, at Galbraith's Ale House in Auckland and at other outlets as far south as Wellington. The aim of owners George and Debbie Craddock, who bought the brewery in 2000, is to brew good-quality 'patio' beer that will satisfy both the islanders and the many tourists who visit during the year and who are seeking a food and drink experience unique to Waiheke. The beers are

ADDRESS
82 Onetangi Road, Onetangi, Waiheke Island

PHONE/FAX
(09) 372 1014

EMAIL
manager@ onetangiroad.co.nz

WEBSITE
www.waihekebrewery. co.nz

BREWER
Andrew Larsen

sold under the Baroona label, Baroona being the name of a ferry that plied the Auckland–Waiheke route for many years. If visiting the island, just ask for the 'Baroona Boys' and everyone will immediately know who and what it is you want! In addition to the beers listed below, the brewery produces two other beers, Baroona Weiss and Full Malty. Unfortunately, try as I might, I could not find any of these to taste.

BAROONA ORIGINAL

ALCOHOL
4.7% abv

STYLE
Lager

Baroona Original is yellow-gold in colour and has a mild malt and citrus aroma. The texture is smooth and clean with medium to full mouth-feel. The flavour evokes malt fruitiness with some citrus — grapefruit, in particular. There is some hop very mildly evident, although it is more floral and lemony than bitter. There is reasonable finish with a pleasant dryness on the back palate. A very big seller, this is a nicely balanced beer with wide appeal. I would serve it with most spicy foods — perhaps a Thai chicken curry.

BAROONA DARK ALE

ALCOHOL
4% abv

STYLE
Dark Lager

This is a dark, red-brown beer that, complete with creamy head, looks attractive in the glass. It has a really chocolatey bouquet and there is some malt fruit there as well to sweeten the aroma. It's not as creamy as some dark beers; rather, it is crisp and clean with good mouth-feel. The flavour is predominantly chocolate as well, but there is enough hop there to provide a balancing dryness/bitterness on the back. It is in the porter style and the lighter texture works to carry the flavour. It is tempting to serve it with Waiheke Island oysters, but I would go further and make up a seafood platter that includes lashings of fresh crayfish.

BEER QUOTES 'Beer has long been the prime lubricant in our social intercourse and the sacred throat-anointing fluid that accompanies the ritual of mateship. To sink a few cold ones with the blokes is both an escape and a confirmation of belonging.' Rennie Ellis (1940–)

BEAN ROCK BREWING COMPANY

ADDRESS
79 Ardmore Road,
PO Box 46-266,
Herne Bay,
Auckland

PHONE
(09) 376 3222

FAX
(09) 376 3735

BREWER
Tony Denny

Thousands of litres of beer went down the drain before Bean Rock Lager was pronounced fit for the market by entrepreneur Richard Holden. Produced at Independent Brewery under the steady hand of brewmaster Tony Denny, Bean Rock Lager is in the genre of European-style lagers. Named after an icon of Auckland's Waitemata harbour, Bean Rock is widely available in packaged form from retail outlets throughout the country.

BEAN ROCK LAGER

ALCOHOL
4.5% abv

STYLE
Lager

Mid-straw in colour and with a hop and citrus aroma, this beer has broad appeal. The texture is clean and crisp and there is good mouth-feel and good length. On the palate it is moderately bitter with some fruit and cut-grass influences, as well as a touch of citrus towards the end. There is also enough residual sweetness to offer good balance, although the hop promise of the aroma does not last long enough to satisfy the real hop-head — the Original Bitter version of the same beer is more likely to please that lot. It's a good beer to enjoy with hot and spicy food — say, Cajun chicken.

THE LOADED HOG BREWERY

ADDRESS
Viaduct Harbour,
104 Quay Street,
Auckland City

PHONE
(09) 379 5395

BREWER
Mike McLean

OPEN
The restaurant and bar is open 11 am– late daily

The Loaded Hog is New Zealand's biggest restaurant/bar group, with outlets in a number of towns. Each venue is strongly themed with a stylish décor focusing on rural New Zealand. The group prides itself on fast, efficient service in an environment that is lively and inviting. A full menu is available at each venue and an integral feature of each bar is the award-winning range of beers. The on-tap range is the same in each venue, and pigoon (the Loaded Hog's quirky name for riggers or PETs) and keg sales are available. The Auckland brewery, located away from the

BEER QUOTES 'Instead of water we got here a draught of beer, . . . a lumberer's drink, which would acclimate and naturalize a man at once, — which would make him see green, and, if he slept, dream that he heard the wind sough among the pines.' Henry David Thoreau (1817–62)

restaurant, services the Loaded Hogs in Auckland, Hamilton and in Wellington, as well as One Red Dog restaurants in Auckland, Takapuna and two sites in Wellington. The Christchurch brewery (page 124) supplies South Island venues.

Loaded Hog beers are also available from selected supermarkets and retail outlets in packaged form. These are made at the Steam Brewing Company in Auckland and vary slightly from the draught versions made at Loaded Hog sites.

HOG GOLD LAGER

ALCOHOL
4% abv

STYLE
Lager

Yellow-gold, the colour of dry hay, this very popular lager has a mild aroma of grass, honey and hay. The body, in true American lager fashion, is crisp and clean, and there is no great finish. The flavour is mild, with some honey sweetness and a very slight hop bitterness. It's an easy-drinking, mildly flavoured offering that is sure to have a large following. Uncomplicated and inoffensive, it is a well-made example of its style and a good food beer. I would serve it with a mild curry or a generous bowl of chilli con carne.

HOG DRAFT BEER

ALCOHOL
4% abv

STYLE
New Zealand
Draught

An inviting, dark brown colour and a thick, creamy head provide the first impressions of this mainstream Kiwi draught. There is a mild malt sweetness to the aroma, with evidence of Christmas fruit mince. The mouth-feel is generous, while the texture is crisp and clean. Malt sweetness dominates the flavour but a distinct dryness on the back palate adds a dimension. This is a well-balanced beer with obvious appeal to the average Kiwi brown-beer drinker. It is pleasant drinking at the best of times, but for added pleasure serve it with a hearty roast beef sandwich with pickles, mustard and all the trimmings!

HOG DARK ALE

Very dark ruby in colour with a thick, creamy head, this beer has an aroma that is full of chocolate with additional mild molasses and coffee influences. It has a medium texture, creamy with a slightly grainy mouth-feel. It's fresh and mouth-filling, with dark fruit flavours and suggestions of molasses, and yeast and Marmite characters. This is a good example of a dark beer with the texture to carry the flavours through to the back palate. Serve it with black pudding or, for a contrast, fresh Orongo Bay oysters.

ALCOHOL
4% abv

STYLE
Dark Lager

AWARDS
Bronze Medal, Dark Ale, Australian International Beer Awards 2003

HOG WHEAT BEER

The brewer tells me this orange-gold beer is the favourite of Loaded Hog staff. It has no great aromatics but there is evidence of some tropical fruit and a hint of barley/wheat, as well as some biscuit influence (which may be why the young staff like it!). Very soft in texture and equally mild in flavour, it has no great length. It offers little challenge to the palate but is an easy drink at any time of the year. It's hard to pick a food that won't overpower it, but try whole fish (snapper or hoki) baked with some slices of lemon and seasoned with freshly ground pepper.

ALCOHOL
4% abv

STYLE
Filtered Wheat Beer

HOG BLONDE PILSNER BEER

A pale straw colour with a cut-grass aroma, a little green, a little hoppy. It has a light body, crisp and clean, and is moderately flavoured with a base of malt and a touch of fruitiness. It has only a touch of bitterness tending to be more tart than hoppy. It is an easy-drinking summer beer that will adequately quench the thirst. I would serve it up with shellfish or with steak and salad or even spicy tacos when it will keep the palate clean and alive.

ALCOHOL
5.5% abv

STYLE
New World Pilsner

HOG LIGHT BEER

A low-alcohol beer typical of many with almost no aroma, a very light body and only subtle flavour. It is difficult to make an appealing light beer and like most others this could do with a little more in the

ALCOHOL
2.2% abv

STYLE
Low-strength Lager

middle palate to keep it in balance. I believe the brewer when he tells me this is popular in the Loaded Hog bars, as for the designated driver or those looking for a low-strength beer this is a solid if unchallenging option. Use it to wash down any meal but it is unlikely to provide a discussion point for those looking for the perfect match.

SHAKESPEARE TAVERN & BREWERY

ADDRESS
61 Albert Street,
Auckland City

PHONE
(09) 373 5396

FAX
(09) 373 5397

BREWER
Barry Newman

OPEN
Mon–Fri 11.30 am–
late
Sat 12 noon–late

TASTINGS
By request

The Shakespeare brewery is in the Shakespeare Tavern, one of central Auckland's older licensed premises and owned by publican Ron Urlich. It is the site of New Zealand's first modern minibrewery, and brewing takes place right in front of bar patrons. Long-time brewer Barry Newman is considered a doyen of craft brewing in New Zealand. Barry is astute enough to understand what his patrons want in a beer and clever enough to brew beer that rises well above the average and he introduces his regulars and many tourists to a variety of beer styles. He uses a traditional batch-brewing process to ensure a continuous supply of unfiltered and non-pasteurised beers for patrons.

I have enjoyed Barry's beers on many occasions, no less so than most recently when I visited them again to update this guide. I think the aspects that most appeal are the consistent quality and the variation of styles in the range. Barry's beers are always great subjects for conversation with other beer drinkers.

Ask about Barry's seasonal and special beers when visiting the Shakespeare. The beer is also available to take away in 2-litre PETs.

BARRACLOUGH LAGER

ALCOHOL
4.1% abv

STYLE
European-style
Lager

A bright straw-gold in colour, this lager is highly aromatic with lots of hop influence and some grassy notes — most likely from the dry hopping used in its production. The texture is crisp and clean, while the flavour is sweetish to begin with, then filled with hop flavour and with plenty of residual hop bitterness on the finish. It is stored for two months before release to enhance its mellowness. It's a well-balanced, fresh-tasting beer with full and generous use of hops making it ideal with food. Serve it up with braised lamb shanks or, for something lighter, battered fish and chips.

BOHEMIAN LAGER

A smooth rather than crisp lager, the Bohemian is very drinkable, with a rich, malty base and a touch of botanicals giving it a grassy aroma and a moderately herbal flavour combined with a citrus tang. There is a pleasant bitterness on the back of the palate that has a nicely spicy finish. I would match this with a creamy fettuccine or perhaps with an Asian dish such as chilli prawns.

ALCOHOL
5% abv

STYLE
Bohemian-style
Lager

SHYLOCK'S LIGHT ALE

This good quaffing beer is a sparkling copper-gold colour with a malty aroma that has some molasses character. In the mouth it is crisp and clean with plenty of freshness. The malt comes through as flavour as well, but there is plenty of hop there, too — and a touch of ginger and spice to boot. Overall, this is a very well-balanced, lower strength beer with good mouth-feel and a tight, dry finish. Don't be faint-hearted with your food match: this beer will stand a solid, red meat meal. Odds on, it will go great with Mexican tacos or burritos.

ALCOHOL
3% abv

STYLE
Light Ale

SHAKESPEARE DRAUGHT

An appealing yellow-gold colour and a very mild aroma make this an interesting beer from the start. Best described as a mainstream draught, it has a smooth texture and creamy mouth-feel. There is plenty of malt character in the flavour but it is not overly sweet, with good hop influence as well. There is fruit but it doesn't dominate and the result is a pleasing and popular New Zealand brown-beer style with no great length that is great at a barbecue and equally at home with a winter hotpot.

ALCOHOL
4% abv

STYLE
New Zealand
Draught

MACBETH'S RED ALE

ALCOHOL	4% abv
STYLE	Red Ale

Ruby-red with a mild malt aroma, this beer in the Scottish style is crisp with a reasonably dominant malt fruity base with some floral notes. But the real point of interest is the character the hops seem to impart. I would describe it as a soft sourness, not quite a citrus touch, which is appealing but might not be to everyone's liking. It's a fascinating beer for the more adventurous draught drinkers. With its ability to cut through the palate it is another good Shakespeare food beer — a piece of gently grilled Scotch fillet or a venison steak will make an excellent match or perhaps shellfish with a splash of the beer in the pot.

FALSTAFF'S REAL ALE

ALCOHOL	4.3% abv
STYLE	English-style Bitter

 TOP BREW

In the glass this is a red-gold beer with a thick, creamy head. It is highly aromatic, with hops taking centre stage and some tropical fruit waiting in the wings. It is fresh and creamy in texture and the mouth-feel is generous. You immediately taste the sweetish fruit influence, some caramel and the abundant hop bitterness as well. It is a complex bittersweet beer, with well-balanced flavours and an excellent, satisfying finish that some describe as cedary and molasses-like. I really like this beer and look forward to serving it with duck roasted with stone fruit.

PISTOLS OLD SOLDIER ALE

ALCOHOL	6.3% abv
STYLE	Dark Ale

 TOP BREW

This was the first time I had tasted this beer and its appeal was immediately obvious. It looks good in the glass and has a roasted-malt dominated aroma that captures Christmas fruit mince and caramel. The flavour mirrors the aroma, with some malt fruitiness and some mild sherry-like tastes as well. The higher alcohol content provides a good vehicle for the flavour and the overall effect is of a satisfying brew full of flavour and texture. Enjoy it before a meal when it is sure to stimulate the taste buds or as an after-dinner warmer.

WILLPOWER STOUT

ALCOHOL
4% abv

STYLE
Stout

 **TOP BREW**

This English-style stout is a very dark, almost black beer with a thick, creamy head. In contrast to previous tastings, this had a strongly caramel aroma with just a hint of molasses and fruit mince. The texture is light and crisp with a freshness that's appealing. The flavour is malty with some roasted- and bitter-chocolate influences. Soft coffee hints are also there, with the caramel making another appearance just to keep things interesting. Willpower Stout has good flavour balance, although it is the texture that sets this example of the style apart. As this stout is good with cheese, consider serving it with a blue-cheese soufflé.

KING LEAR OLD ALE

ALCOHOL
8% abv

STYLE
Old Ale

Full-bodied, full-strength and full-on, this beer, with a little higher alcohol content than I recall from my last visit, is not for the faint-hearted! It is a deep, deep amber-brown with a thick, creamy head. The aroma is quite mild, with malt sweetness coming through, as well as some Marmite character. The texture is thick, rich and creamy. The flavour is full and sweet on the front — some toffee, some chocolate — with nicely balanced hop bitterness on the back. A thoroughly pleasant supping ale to enjoy before a meal, it is equally good as a fireside finish to an evening.

LION BREWERIES

ADDRESS
111 Carlton Gore Rd, Newmarket, Auckland

PHONE
(09) 377 8840

FAX
(09) 358 8587

WEBSITE
www.lion-nathan.co.nz

Five breweries come under the umbrella of Lion Breweries New Zealand: Wellington Brewing Company (see page 66), Mac's (see page 81), Canterbury Brewery (see page 123), Speight's (see page 145), and Lion Breweries in Newmarket, Auckland. The Great Northern Brewery, as Lion Breweries was first called, was established in 1860 over a spring in Newmarket by Richard Seccombe, who used the lion from his family crest on the logo. Lion Breweries was established after a merger between the Great

Northern and Albert Breweries in 1915, and in 1958 a modern brewing plant was built on the current Auckland site. Lion Breweries is New Zealand's largest brewer, with a capacity over all its breweries of around 1.6 million hectolitres. A number of Lion products are brewed and packaged in Newmarket and the other sites for local and overseas markets. Some brands are brewed at more than one site. The company brews a number of international brands under licence, and Stella Artois is one of these.

Lion employs over 600 full-time permanent staff across New Zealand and contributes substantial funds to community and sporting projects throughout the country.

ADDRESS
380 Khyber Pass Road, Newmarket, Auckland

LIONZONE
A state-of-the-art exhibition of brewing and the history of Lion Breweries.

PHONE
(09) 358 8366

TOURS
9.30 am, 12.15 pm & 3 pm daily
Bookings essential

ICE

A very pale straw colour, Ice has a fruity, sweet aroma. It is very light in texture, clean and smooth. Designed for uncomplicated, easy drinking, its flavour is also relatively sweet and floral with a short finish. Ice is a beer in the modern style, aimed at the drinker looking for a light, quaffing beverage, and it numbers among its fans many who do not consider themselves beer drinkers. The subtle flavour is good for any simple seafood dish, but it is also an ideal contrast to hot and spicy Indian curries, calming the palate.

ALCOHOL
4.7% abv

STYLE
Lager

LIGHT ICE

Light Ice is a low-alcohol beer that is pale straw in colour with a distinctively floral and fruity aroma. The crisp texture and very little mouth-feel give it a refreshing quality. The flavour is full, sweet and floral with a little spiciness at the end. There is some mild hop flavour present that adds weight. It is a complement to spicy ethnic foods or a safe bet on its own.

ALCOHOL
2.5% abv

STYLE
Low-strength Lager

> **BEER FACTS** English prisoners who were sentenced to hanging were taken from the prison to the gallows on a wagon. Along the way the prisoner was allowed to go into a pub for a pint. Hence the terms 'on the wagon' and 'off the wagon'.

LION RED

ALCOHOL	4% abv
STYLE	New Zealand Draught

For a long time New Zealand's biggest-selling beer, Lion Red more or less defines the Kiwi brown-beer style. It is mid-brown in colour and has a smooth, mouth-filling texture. The aroma is malty with some evidence of fruit, while the flavour is full of malt sweetness balanced by a moderate hop bitterness in the mid-palate. It has a good length and a mild aftertaste. This is a hugely popular beer best served fresh from the tap and enjoyed with any red meat dish — its robust maltiness is a good match with the full flavour of a rich, hearty casserole.

RHEINECK LAGER

ALCOHOL	4% abv
STYLE	Lager

Its name may sound German, but Rheineck has a long Kiwi heritage. Born at the now-closed Waikato Breweries in Hamilton, this lager-style beer is light tan-gold in colour and has a malt fruit aroma. The texture is slightly creamy and it is smooth, with good body. The hop character is understated on the palate and its sweetish, malty character is more dominant — overall, it is a 'softer' beer for those who like the rounder finish. Rheineck makes a subtle companion to complex Southeast Asian cuisine like satay prawns.

WAIKATO DRAUGHT

ALCOHOL	4% abv
STYLE	New Zealand Draught

A persistent favourite, Waikato Draught is golden-brown in colour with a combination of fruit, hop and spice in the aroma. The texture is smooth and clean and the mouth-feel is generous. The taste is comparatively weighty, with malt and hop both contributing flavour. There is an element of bitterness to Waikato that carries the flavour into an easy drinking finish. This means it is a good match for a hearty meat-and-potatoes meal and, without a doubt, that piece of sirloin just off the barbecue.

STEINLAGER

ALCOHOL	5% abv
STYLE	Lager

An icon on the New Zealand beer scene, Steinlager has many supporters among those who like a hoppier tipple. It is light brown with a slight lime hue in the glass. The aroma is dry with plenty of

Green Bullet hops evident, and some hay and garden herb characters come through. It is full flavoured with plenty of mouth-feel, a distinctive grassy note and a dry, astringent finish. It is a challenging beer for some but offers a real alternative to the sweet Kiwi brown-beer style. Steinlager complements any dish that includes herbs, particularly Mediterranean food. Try it with rare smoked beef with a sun-dried tomato pesto.

STEINLAGER PREMIUM LIGHT

ALCOHOL
2.5% abv

STYLE
Low-strength Lager

Traditionally, low-alcohol beers have failed to gain ascendancy in the New Zealand market. However, Steinlager Premium Light has succeeded better than most. It's certainly not as full as regular Steinlager but it does retain the grassy, herbaceous characters that make its full-strength parent so distinctive. The brewers have also succeeded in ensuring Steinlager Light has more than a modicum of the Steinlager bitterness, setting it apart from any lifeless, run-of-the-mill competitors.

STELLA ARTOIS

ALCOHOL
5.2% abv

STYLE
Pilsner

Stella Artois (or simply Stella, as it is known to many of its fans) is a pilsner-style beer that originated in Belgium and is now brewed and consumed the world over. It's pale gold in colour with a fruity/floral aroma. It has a crisp, clean texture, a mildly grassy flavour, a moderate level of bitterness on the top palate and an attractive, hoppy finish. It's an easy-drinking, well-balanced beer for the masses, without significant challenge. The New Zealand brew is pleasant enough when fresh and has the refined dryness looked for in a beer of this style. I would serve it with traditional Belgian fare of steamed mussels or fries and mayonnaise — or fresh crusty bread and a slab of Gruyère for good measure.

LION PILS

ALCOHOL
4% abv

STYLE
Pale Lager

Lion Pils is a standard pale gold lager targeted very precisely at the 'emerging drinker' market, so it is an easy-drinking brew, light in texture and light in taste. It has a slightly citrus tang provided by the liberal use of Saaz hops. There is no perceivable lingering bitterness and this beer appeals most to those who shy away from strong aftertaste or to those just starting out on the journey to find a beer style they enjoy. It is packaged in bottles with hip purple and orange branding. In addition, this beer has its very own interactive website for the young at heart. Look it up on www.pilsman.co.nz.

GALBRAITH BREWING COMPANY

Galbraith's Ale House opened in June 1995 and has been developing a constantly expanding coterie of devotees ever since. These are beer drinkers who seldom go anywhere else and who can blame them. A range of English-style 'real ales' is brewed and served on site; brewer Keith Galbraith's attention to detail in pursuit of authenticity is amazing. All the beers are top-fermented, unfiltered and non-pasteurised, and are cask conditioned to boot. They are served without carbonation, straight from the conditioning casks, by hand pump, at a cellar temperature of 10–12°C. The result is a complete range of beer that is full and strong and ideal for savouring with others who appreciate its quality.

I get to Galbraith's as often as I can but each time I regret not having visited more often. Consistent since it opened, Galbraith's continues to offer a total experience: wonderful ambience, great food and outstanding beers, among which even the most familiar, surprisingly, just keep getting better. Keith Galbraith, a quiet and unassuming individual, seems to have an innate ability to first tempt and then please the palate.

His beers are not overly full of alcohol but they are so well made and presented they leave you with the impression of having had a substantial drinking session for great value. Keith Galbraith is a true innovator in New Zealand craft brewing and while there

ADDRESS
2 Mount Eden Road, Mount Eden, Auckland

PHONE
(09) 379 3557

FAX
(09) 307 6721

EMAIL
real.ale@xtra.co.nz

BREWERS
Keith Galbraith & Ian Ramsey

OPEN
Sun–Wed 12 noon–11 pm
Thu–Sat 12 noon–midnight

are some in the industry who try desperately to mimic the Galbraith style they are nowhere near as good, invariably failing to match the careful and thoughtful choice of ingredients and the expressive nature of their use in the brewing process.

In spite of the emergence of a plethora of theme bars, the Auckland home of the range, Galbraith's Ale House, remains unique to New Zealand and is testimony to the passion and effort Keith puts into his craft. The Galbraith beers, as well as a full menu, are available at the Ale House, as is a selection of draught and packaged brews representing some of the best New Zealand — and the world — has to offer.

BOB HUDSON'S BITTER

ALCOHOL
4% abv
STYLE
Standard Bitter

Rose-gold with a thick, creamy head, this smooth-as-silk bitter has delightful aromatics: citrus and honey with full malt and lashings of tropical fruit influences, including mango and banana. The texture is rich and creamy and the flavour is complex with sweet and floral characters sitting easily with plenty of hop bitterness and bite. It's an easy-drinking ale made with Maris Otter and crystal malts and Goldings hops, sure to please those with a preference for hop aroma and taste. Antipasto would bring out the complexity of this beer; for a simpler option, try grilled pork chops with just a touch of applesauce.

BELLRINGERS BITTER

ALCOHOL
4.5% abv
STYLE
Best Bitter

 TOP BREW

A burnished copper, almost amber colour and a creamy, white head characterise this beer named after a group of regular customers. There are ripe berryfruit influences in the aroma, together with chocolate-malt notes. The texture is soft, the mouth-feel full and fresh and it is this that makes an immediate impact. A well-balanced blend of malt sweetness that provides a gentle fruitiness and a lingering hop bitterness best describes the flavour, which is probably why this beer is the biggest seller across the Galbraith's bar. I'd serve it in true English fashion — with classic toad-in-the-hole.

GRAFTON PORTER

ALCOHOL
4.5% abv
STYLE
Stout/Porter

'A full-bodied dark ale' are the words brewer Keith Galbraith uses to describe this beer, which is indeed an accurate way to summarise its almost black colour and full, creamy texture. The aroma is mild, with a little coffee and caramel in the bouquet. The use of roasted and chocolate malts without doubt provides the basis of its lovely, malty flavour, which lingers long and strong, meandering gently, confidently across the palate. Hop lovers should have no fear — the bitterness is there to keep the balance. True class in a glass. Try it with a selection of cheese for a long summer lunch, or a rich stout and Stilton soup by the fireside in cooler months.

BITTER AND TWISTED

ALCOHOL
5% abv
STYLE
English-style Bitter

TOP BREW

This remains my favourite of Keith Galbraith's range of quite exceptional beers. Mid-amber in colour with a malt fruit and tobacco aroma, a smooth, creamy texture and a generous, well-balanced, bittersweet flavour profile, this beer can be enjoyed at any time of day or year. The quality of the ingredients shines through, each being allowed to stand on its merits while contributing wonderfully to the whole in a distinguished country lodge rather than a Las Vegas manner. It has everything I seek in a beer: aromatics, texture and body, balanced flavours and plenty of character to keep me interested. The high alcohol content means it is a great palate stimulator, but if seeking a menu partner I'd opt for quail, roasted in a stout and berryfruit sauce and served with a selection of root vegetables. However, for a much simpler combo you could try the simply delicious Galbraith's battered fish and chips.

BOHEMIAN PILSNER

ALCOHOL
4.3% abv
STYLE
Czech-style Pilsner

This is an incredibly drinkable lager in the style of old Czechoslovakian pilsners. A delicious aroma of spice and hop and fresh fruit wafts from the glass. The taste is bittersweet with a grassy dryness that is both appealing and cleansing, and a super dry/bitter finish. This colourful pilsner is made using specially imported hops, but while it is truly hoppy the balancing influence of the Pilsner and Vienna malts is clearly evident and makes for a well-balanced, enjoyable session beer. I favour hearty, meat-dominant food with this beer, which adds sweetness for balance and bitterness to keep the palate awake.

RESURRECTION TRAPPIST STYLE ALE

ALCOHOL
8% abv

STYLE
Trappist-style Ale

TOP BREW

From the moment you lift the glass to your nose the spicy character of this beautiful beer is evident. Exquisitely presentable, with its creamy, white head, this beer will delight you. The slightly medicinal/herbal/spicy/malty flavour carried by a rich, velvety texture glides across the palate settling comfortably in every nook and cranny as if it owns your mouth. This is certainly a beer for supping and savouring. I rate it among the top beers in the country and would suggest resisting any attempt to cloud its marvellous qualities with food, choosing instead to enjoy it quietly in its singular glory.

TRIDENT TAVERN

ADDRESS
69 Selwyn Street, Onehunga, Auckland

PHONE
(09) 636 9070

FAX
(09) 622 0764

BREWER
Tavita Lefale

OPEN
Mon–Wed 10 am–11 pm
Thu–Sat 10 am–1 am
Sun Lounge bar open 11 am–8.30 pm

The Trident Tavern is a reasonably large, established complex in the Auckland suburb of Onehunga. As well as a number of bars, it has a well-patronised liquor store and, uncommonly for this style of operation, a small brewery. The brewery supplies the hotel and patrons who want to take beer home. Owned by Fatu Fuatavai, the tavern is the meeting place for a host of locals who come to enjoy the camaraderie and the atmosphere. The beers are mainstream and obviously appeal to the many patrons, each of whom has his or her clear favourite. The selection is wide and varied, with some common brewing themes running through.

TRIDENT PUB LAGER

ALCOHOL
4% abv

STYLE
Lager

A pale gold colour and a very mild malt aroma form the first impressions of this session lager. The texture is lightweight with little mouth-feel and a short finish. There is some malt influence in the flavour, along with some citrus character, but it is a dryness that may come from the hops that is the most obvious feature. On the day this felt like a very young beer, which may explain its texture and dryness. It would be difficult to match it with a food that didn't overwhelm it — fish is probably best.

TRIDENT PUB DRAUGHT

This beer is the colour of golden syrup — a deep golden brown. The aroma reminds me of the inside of a freezer, while the texture is light and clean. There are some light malt flavours as well as a little hop character. This is particularly dry, brown quaffing beer with a short finish, suitable for serving at a barbecue or around a campfire.

ALCOHOL
4% abv

STYLE
New Zealand
Draught

TRIDENT ICE BEER

Another pale gold offering, this one has a distinct apple-cider aroma. There is medium mouth-feel and a lightweight texture to carry the flavour. The predominant taste is the malt, which is most likely responsible for the residual sweetness. In this beer the hop influence is more pronounced and so is the dryness/bitterness that characterises many of the Trident brews. This is a good summer session beer best served with beer and garlic sausages hot off the grill.

ALCOHOL
4% abv

STYLE
Lager

TRIDENT SUPER

This is my pick of the Trident brews. It is gold with a lime hue and an aroma of tropical fruit with some spiciness. The texture is crisp and clean. It has medium mouth-feel and good length. The balance between malt and hop is welcome and there is a hint of caramel in the flavour to keep it interesting. There is a degree of hop bitterness on the back palate, giving this beer a 'drink me' character. Partner with spicy tortillas or any other dish that has some fire to it.

ALCOHOL
4% abv

STYLE
Lager

TRIDENT PUB DARK

Pub Dark is actually a reddish-brown colour. While there is no aroma to speak of, the texture is creamy and smooth. It has a mild flavour combining some roasted malt character with a bit of coffee and some

ALCOHOL
4% abv

STYLE
Dark Lager

toffee to boot. Another offering with some residual hop bitterness resulting in an extended length of flavour, it is more a Kiwi brown beer than a dark beer, but all the same it's a welcome variation in the Trident range. Save it for the hearty meat pie occasion.

WAITEMATA BREWERY (DB BREWERIES)

DB Breweries, part of DB Group Ltd, maintains four breweries at Waitemata, Mangatainoka (Tui Brewery, see page 59), Greymouth (Monteith's Brewing Company, see page 89) and Timaru (Mainland Brewery, see page 137). William Coutts opened the original Waitemata Brewery in Auckland in 1930. After World War II the brewery underwent considerable expansion. In 1950 Coutts's son, Morton, began research on the continuous-fermentation method of brewing. This replaced the previously used batch system, allowing a flow of ingredients in the fermentation.

In 1988 DB Breweries became part of Magnum Corporation, one of two major New Zealand liquor and food distribution corporations. In late 1992 Magnum was renamed DB Group. Today, the major shareholding is held by Heineken. The company is a major supporter of a variety of community, sporting and cultural activities around New Zealand. DB beers are available as packaged product and on tap from bars, restaurants and retail liquor stores throughout the country.

ADDRESS
Cnr Bairds & Great South Roads, Otahuhu, Auckland

PHONE
(09) 259 3000

FAX
(09) 259 3001

WEBSITE
www.db.co.nz

HEAD BREWER
Dave Eaton

TOURS
Tue–Fri 10.30 am

DB BITTER

DB Bitter is a full-flavoured, mainstream New Zealand brown beer sold mostly in cans from liquor retailers. It has a malt fruit aroma with a hint of grain and grassiness. The texture when the beer is well chilled is crisp and clean and the flavour has an acceptable balance of malt sweetness and hop. It's an easy-drinking session beer with good

ALCOHOL
3.5% abv

STYLE
New Zealand Draught

mouth-feel and a moderately sweet/bitter finish. It is the perfect beer for everyday dishes at home or when eating out. Serve it with curried sausages or with dishes that will benefit from the fruity sweetness it will bring to the combination.

DOUBLE BROWN

Historically a very popular standard bearer for DB, Double Brown is available nationwide in draught or packaged form. It is a deep copper-brown colour and should pour with a generous, creamy head. It has a malty aroma that provides a fresh introduction to a sweetish, full-flavoured beer. The texture is creamy and fills the mouth; the taste is malty and dark caramel-like, with some bittersweet character. It's easy drinking in the Kiwi brown-beer style, albeit slightly more substantial than many. Enjoy with heartier red meat meals.

ALCOHOL
4% abv

STYLE
New Zealand
Draught

EXPORT DRY

Export Dry has a golden grain colour and a cut-grass and tropical-fruit aroma that implies freshness. It has good mouth-feel and a dryish texture that becomes crisper when the beer is served well chilled. There is very moderate hop influence, with the overall impression being a malt fruit sweetness. On the finish there is a residual sweetness that, together with a welcome late hint of hop, provides some length. This is an award-winning beer in its category and most suited as an accompaniment to flavour-driven food, perfect to cool the palate after forays into the spices of the Orient and the Middle East when it will add a balancing sweetness. Go for curry or for spicy lamb kebabs!

ALCOHOL
5% abv

STYLE
Lager

EXPORT GOLD

Export Gold is a deep golden, full-strength lager with a fresh, mild hop and malt aroma. On the palate it is refreshing and smooth with good mouth-filling qualities. The flavour is moderately malty with some pleasant biscuity influences. It has a well-balanced, lengthy finish derived from the second addition of hops. This is sold as a premium beer that, like many easy-drinking sweetish lagers, is ideal for pairing with spicy Thai, Indonesian and Indian cuisines.

ALCOHOL
4% abv

STYLE
Golden Lager

HEINEKEN

ALCOHOL
5% abv
STYLE
Lager

Heineken is brewed by DB Breweries in New Zealand under licence. Strict quality control ensures the features that make this a universally admired brew are matched in the local version. A mid-gold colour with a slight lime tinge, Heineken has a hoppy aroma with some freshly milled grain character. The texture is rich and smooth, the flavour full with a slightly fruity yet mildly bitter taste, and there is a good level of effervescence. It has good length with a welcome hop bitterness of moderate strength. It is a great accompaniment to shellfish, light chicken dishes and herb-influenced pasta. Try it with seafood linguine!

FLAME BEER

ALCOHOL
5.2% abv
STYLE
Lager

This beer was originally produced by Black Dog Breweries, one of DB Breweries' marketing inventions. It has a very loyal following, especially in the urban café and club scene. I cannot remember it leaving much of an impression in the past but this time around it showed better form in the DB line-up. It is a bright gold colour with a moderately floral, sweet fruit aroma. It is smooth rather than crisp but clean and refreshing, best drunk quite cold. The flavour has elements of honey and tropical fruit with enough bite to keep it interesting. While it has moderate length, there is plenty of flavour on the back palate. Enjoy it as an easy-drinking session beer that is likely to suit most occasions.

AMSTEL LIGHT

ALCOHOL
2.5% abv
STYLE
Low-strength Lager

When the occasion calls for a low-alcohol beer Amstel Light, like its full-strength sister brewed under licence by DB Breweries, is a perfectly valid option. It is available in bottles and is a pale straw colour. It has medium body with more generous mouth-weight than expected for light beer. It has a fresh, fruity taste with an admirable balance of fruit and malt flavours. It is slightly spritzy, made more refreshing by the cold filtration it undergoes to counter the fewer antioxidants lower alcohol beer has to keep it fresh. There is also enough bitterness on the finish to remind the cynical that this is a true beer.

AMSTEL BEER

ALCOHOL
5% abv

STYLE
Lager

DB Breweries have brewed Amstel under licence since 1997. You will find this only in draught form in bars and cafés; the packaged beer is still imported. It is pale gold in colour with a very subtle aroma that shows fruity malt and some cereal character. The mouth-feel is light and spritzy, and the taste sweetish malt with only the slightest hop bitterness in flavour. This is a well-made, easy-drinking thirst quencher rather than anything too challenging for the palate. I would serve it with antipasto or spicy Thai fish cakes.

STEAM BREWING COMPANY

ADDRESS
186 James Fletcher Drive, Otahuhu, Auckland

PHONE
(09) 270 1890

FAX
(09) 270 1893

EMAIL
luke@steam.brewing.co.nz

BREWER
Luke Nicholas

OPEN
Cock & Bull outlets Daily 12 noon–late

The Steam Brewing Company is the brewing arm of a business that includes five English-style pubs, one in Auckland's eastern suburbs, one in Ellerslie, others in Newmarket and in Lynfield, as well as another in Hamilton. These all operate under the Cock & Bull English Pub brand and all of them serve Steam Brewing Company beers.

The company, including the brewery, was opened in 1995 and since then has become firmly established and patronised by a loyal group of patrons. The site of the first Cock & Bull in East Tamaki is now the company headquarters while the brewery now occupies the site that was formerly Auckland Brewing Company. All the company beers are made there and distributed to the Cock & Bull outlets. In recent years new beers have been added to the range and changes have been made in the recipes of others to reflect the tastes of the production team and the company's customers.

Brewer Luke Nicholas, with the support of Cock & Bull

BEER FACTS Developed in 18th-century England, porter was a mixed beer drink containing three different beers. Sometimes called 'three threads', it required the bartender to blend tankards from three separate taps.

owner Kieran Meyer, sticks to a successful philosophy of constantly adapting the beers to create the ultimate tipple. At the same time he seeks to develop broader interest in beer by offering a selection of unusual styles and seasonal beers. The brewery's beers have won many awards and continue to delight a large band of customers who travel from near and far to enjoy the beer and the atmosphere of the Cock & Bull. A full lunch and dinner menu is available at each venue.

CLASSIC DRAUGHT

This is an amber-coloured lager, with a hoppy aroma underlined by malt fruit and a light and smooth texture. Its smooth texture takes it from being a mainstream quaffer to a much more interesting beer with more balance and complexity than earlier versions. Gentle malt fruit characters become evident as the beer warms but the hops favoured by the brewer continue to show their influence. It has a much better length making it a well-made session beer with a certain challenge. Try serving it with barbecued calamari.

ALCOHOL
4% abv

STYLE
New Zealand Draught

AWARDS
3 Bronze Medals, Australian International Beer Awards 2004

FUGGLES BEST BITTER

This hand-pulled, tan-gold brown beer is definitely a star in the range. It has a lovely cascade when poured and a generous, creamy head. It has an interesting aroma of Christmas cake with some rose-petal, almost floral, character as well. The texture is creamy and smooth with no obvious carbonation. The flavour is mildly malty at first — and then you get real bitter herb tastes as well. This intense bitterness lasts and lasts but is never biting on the back palate. Of all the beers in the range this is among the most complex and balanced and with the Monks Habit, is at the heart of the brewer's true passion for full-flavoured beers. I really enjoyed it as a total package. I'd have it with lamb chops and mint sauce to add a balancing sweetness.

ALCOHOL
4.5% abv

STYLE
English Best Bitter

AWARDS
Silver Medal, New Zealand Beer Awards 2003
Bronze Medal, New Zealand Beer Awards 2004
3 Silver Medals, Australian International Beer Awards 2004
3 Bronze Medals, Australian International Beer Awards 2004

 TOP BREW

MONKS HABIT ABBEY ALE

Another fuller strength offering, this is a rich golden-brown in colour, and has a full malt fruit aroma with some Christmas cake character as well. On the palate it is creamy and smooth with satisfying mouthfeel. The flavour is well balanced, with sweetish malt and fruit on the front and strong hop flavour on the sides and back, with that high hop bitterness providing the length. After a couple of mouthfuls you also taste soft honey and caramel influences that last and last to the final satisfying drop. Perhaps the most complex and stylistically pure of the brewer's offerings, it is certainly well made and continues to be a pub icon. Enjoy it as an aperitif or use its full flavour to match a hearty roast of beef with a rich, dark gravy.

ALCOHOL
7% abv

STYLE
Abbey Ale

AWARDS
Gold Medal and Best in Class, New Zealand Beer Awards 2003

Best in Class, Australian International Beer Awards 2003

2 Silver Medals, Australian International Beer Awards 2004

4 Gold Medals, Australian International Beer Awards 2004

Gold Medal, New Zealand Beer Awards 2004

 TOP BREW

DARK STAR DARK ALE

Very dark brown in colour, Dark Star has lots of caramel and roasted malt with some biscuit characters in the aroma. The texture is light and smooth with a medium level of creaminess. The taste is initially medium-sweet with roasted malt and some dark chocolate and caramel flavours coming through. Then the very high bitterness and citrus character of Steam Brewing Company brews sets in and stays until the very last, bolstered along by a touch of berryfruit. Its finish is much longer than previously and the flavour carries to the back palate more successfully. It is in the style of a light porter and I would serve it with good-quality aged cheddar or with a nicely robust beef stroganoff.

ALCOHOL
5% abv

STYLE
Dark Ale

AWARDS
Silver Medal, Australian International Beer Awards 2004

Gold Medal, Australian International Beer Awards 2004

BEER QUOTES 'A glass of bitter beer or pale ale taken with the principal meal of the day, does more good and less harm than any medicine the physicians can prescribe.' Dr S. Carpenter, 1750

BLUE GOOSE LAGER

Sweet, fresh aromas are the first thing you notice about this crisp beer, which is a honey-gold in colour. The texture is lightweight but the taste is intense, with some tropical fruit and caramel initially, then tart citrus and hop flavours take over. Unlike previous impressions, this beer seemed far more balanced with the malt and the noble hop working in harmony, especially when chilled. It changes as it warms and the hop intensity diminishes and the texture smooths out. Choose something reasonably sweet as a meal accompaniment, or opt for fried or grilled food when the hop bitterness could work its magic and cleanse the palate.

ALCOHOL
4.6% abv

STYLE
Pilsner

AWARDS
4 Bronze Medals, Australian International Beer Awards 2004

Silver Medal, New Zealand Beer Awards 2004

BUXOM BLONDE WHEAT BEER

Made with 70% wheat, this filtered, clear, wheat beer has a delicate musky aroma with a citrus note showing through. The citrus character continues on the palate, moderated by a tropical fruit influence. It is crisp and clean with a delicate, bittersweet quality. This bitterness is not as pronounced as in Blue Goose, probably because there is more balancing honey sweetness here. Wheat beers have certainly found favour with Kiwi beer drinkers over the last couple of years and this rendition continues to sell well. Try it with shellfish for best effect.

ALCOHOL
4.8% abv

STYLE
Wheat Beer

AWARDS
Bronze Medal, Australian International Beer Awards 2004

Bronze Medal, New Zealand Beer Awards 2003

INDEPENDENT BREWERY

Independent Brewery, New Zealand's third-largest brewery, is a subsidiary of the privately owned Independent Liquor. It produces a number of beers for export and has four products for the local market that are distributed primarily through super-markets and privately owned liquor stores throughout the country. The company claims that with these three products it has about 25% of the local canned-beer market. The Independent Brewery philosophy is to brew mainstream, price-competitive

ADDRESS
35 Hunua Road, Papakura, Auckland

PHONE
(09) 298 3000

FAX
(09) 299 6699

BREWER
Tony Denny

beers that provide a direct alternative to the products of the two major breweries. The philosophy also includes selling only freshly brewed beer, and the brewery will store it for only one to two weeks after packaging before shipping it to customers. The company also brews and packages a number of bespoke beers for customers. For example it makes two beers — Pacific Lager 6% abv and Burmeister 4% abv — for the Mill Group, a privately owned liquor retailer based in New Plymouth.

In addition, the company has the licence to brew Kingfisher 5% abv for United Breweries India and Carling 4.5% for Molson Breweries Canada.

NEW ZEALAND LAGER

A bright yellow-gold colour makes this an attractive beer in the glass. It has a complex aroma, with hints of apple cider, malt, yeast, hops and a mild sweetness all having an influence. The texture is moderately creamy, clean with plenty of mouth-feel. A balance of malt sweetness and hop flavour comes through on the palate, with some grassiness, herb and hay notes also making an appearance. It has good length and is, overall, a very good example of the Kiwi lager style. For a food match I would serve pan-fried fish with tomatoes, spring onions and a touch of garlic.

ALCOHOL
5% abv
STYLE
Golden Lager

RANFURLY DRAUGHT

The colour of this beer is orange-gold and it has a thick, creamy head that lingers. There are touches of tropical fruit and malt as well as yeast in the aroma, while the texture is light and creamy with a generous mouth-feel. It has a mild malt flavour as well as some caramel and toffee influences. On the back palate there is some astringency that offsets the residual sweetness. It is a pleasant, easy-drinking brown beer with a good length. This is an ideal red meat partner, and I would try it with Lancashire hotpot.

ALCOHOL
4% abv
STYLE
New World Draught

BEER FACTS Beer writers have uncovered an old beer recipe for Cock Ale that calls for a rooster to be placed in a bag and put into the mash, presumably to add body and character.

HAÄGEN LAGER

Despite its European-sounding name, this well-made golden lager is locally produced. It has plenty of grassy hop aroma and a crisp, clean mouth-feel. It has plenty of taste with some malt sweetness and a decent dash of hop bitterness. The grassy notes of the aroma are repeated, and there is a very appealing lengthy end to it. It is the best in the range from this brewery and is often sold at a very reasonable price, but only in packaged form. I believe it goes well with Southern fried chicken or even chicken fried rice or a stir-fry.

ALCOHOL
5% abv

STYLE
European-style Lager

TUBORG

This mild pilsner-style beer is a sister beer to the Tuborg Gold (5.5% abv) from Carlsberg Breweries in Denmark that can be found in beer outlets around the world and which is still imported into this country. The Tuborg Green is a light gold colour with little aroma, a light body and a clean texture. It is an easy-drinking beer, gently flavoured with a short finish. The malt and hop influence is there but in an unchallenging way. Team Tuborg up with a mild curry — it will clean and refresh the palate.

ALCOHOL
4.6%

STYLE
Pilsner

SUNSHINE BREWING COMPANY

Sunshine is a little brewery with a big reputation, especially in Gisborne, where locals flock to fill up with their favourite from the interesting range of mainstream beers presented at competitive prices. Brewers Geoff Logan and Gerry Maude are engaging sorts, eager to satisfy the most discerning drinker and, if time permits, happy to discuss their abiding passion — beer. Sunshine beers have won numerous awards. They can be purchased from the brewery itself and are available on tap in selected pubs in the North Island, particularly in the Wellington region. When visiting the brewery ask about any seasonal or special brews they may have on offer. These are always full of interest.

ADDRESS
109 Disraeli Street, Gisborne

PHONE
(06) 867 7777

FAX
(06) 867 1141

EMAIL
gisbornegold@xtra.co.nz

BREWERS
Geoff Logan & Gerry Maude

OPEN
Mon–Sat 9 am–6 pm

GISBORNE GOLD

'Gizzy Gold' — this is bright yellow-gold with a light hop aroma, and is easily Sunshine's most mainstream beer, both locally and with fans throughout the country. Appealing to the lager drinker, it has a good hop/malt balance and is nicely dry with good length. While not stacked full of flavour, it has a hint of hazelnut that adds character and interest. Over the years it has received many awards in both New Zealand and Australia. It is a good partner to spicy food or simply as a summer thirst quencher.

ALCOHOL
4% abv
STYLE
European-style Lager

BLACK MAGIC

This stout is very black with a slightly grainy texture and strong malt/molasses notes in the aroma. It doesn't have the length you might expect — instead, it is light and refreshing and full of flavour, with hints of coffee, tobacco and cooking chocolate. At the finish there is a fascinating hint of praline that is very appealing. This beer, too, has received its fair share of accolades over the years. I would partner it with steak off the barbecue or even a chocolate mousse!

ALCOHOL
5% abv
STYLE
Stout

RESERVE ALE

A new addition since the last tasting, this is a richly coloured, tawny-red colour, with a nice, firm head. It has hints of cocoa in the aroma, a smooth texture and a malty flavour. A thoroughly drinkable rendition of the style, with the added interest of some roasted malt character towards the back palate, and a suggestion of hop bitterness making its presence felt on the finish. One to team up with a hearty casserole.

ALCOHOL
4% abv
STYLE
Tawny Ale

 **TOP BREW**

BEER QUOTES 'Without question, the greatest invention in the history of mankind is beer. Oh, I grant you that the wheel was also a fine invention, but the wheel does not go nearly as well with pizza.' Dave Barry (1947–)

WHITE CLIFFS BREWING COMPANY

ADDRESS
487 Main Road
North (SH 3),
Urenui, Taranaki

PHONE/FAX
(06) 752 3676

EMAIL
info@organicbeer.
co.nz

BREWER
Steve Ekdahl

OPEN
Mon–Sat 9.30 am–
6pm

Between the shores of the Tasman Sea and the summit of Mt Taranaki in the east of the North Island there lies a treasure waiting to be discovered by adventurous ale drinkers in search of the elusive perfect brew.

Based in a rustic rural backwater outside Urenui on the west coast of the North Island is the White Cliffs Brewing Company established in September 1989 by unemployed Taranaki man Mike Johnson who decided to expand his home-brew experience with a brewery in his back garden. By 1998 White Cliffs was brewing 45,000 litres of Mike's Mild Ale per year and had rated a huge mention in Michael Jackson's highly acclaimed book *Beer*. Jackson rated Mike's Mild as a very good and 'rare example of a New World mild'.

Mike has since moved on but current brewery owners Steve Ekdahl and Sharon Cottam have continued the tradition and brew Mike's Mild with the same commitment to purity as always.

Packaged in riggers, stubbies and kegs, Mike's Mild is available in select outlets in Hamilton, Taranaki, Taupo, Wellington, Nelson and Queenstown. In 2004, Steve and Sharon added to the range with a new beer, Mountain Lager, which is all their own concept and has their own distinctive stamp. The brewery has also produced one-off special edition ales, including an English-style bitter, but these are available only direct from the brewery.

MIKE'S MILD ALE

ALCOHOL
4% abv

STYLE
Amber Ale

AWARDS
Silver Medal — Dark
Beer, New Zealand
Beer Awards 2004

One of only seven fully certificated organic beers in New Zealand, and the North Island's only organic beer, this amber-brown brew is non-pasteurised and unfiltered, with an appealing, earthy, mushroomy aroma with a whiff of caramel adding sweetness. It has plenty of body and remains fresh and light from first to last. The flavour is mild on the taste-buds, biscuity and malty. It is complex and full and benefits from the addition of secondary hops fairly late in the process, which gives it a nice hoppy bite. It's a beer that, although technically a lager, will appeal to ale drinkers who have the good fortune to sample this true labour of love. It is good with mushroom fettuccine or a hearty beef hotpot.

MOUNTAIN LAGER

A brother to Mike's Mild, this ale is made with a traditional ale yeast, organic German malt and rainwater. It is a refreshing brew that Steve says will 'appeal to both the full-time outdoorsman and the weary city slicker seeking a taste of the great outdoors'. It is at this time available only from the brewery and I haven't had an opportunity to try it.

ALCOHOL
4% abv
STYLE
Golden Lager

MATES BREWERY

The shareholders in this custom-built brewery, established in 1995, have adopted a straight-up commercial philosophy, giving customers a no-frills draught beer alternative that competes on price and quality with the products of the larger breweries. This large wholesale beer manufacturer provides batch-brewed double-filtered bulk beer to beer outlets and chartered clubs throughout the North Island from Auckland, Thames Valley-Bay of Plenty, across the Central Plateau region and as far south as Wellington. Ninety per cent is sold under the Mates label from selected outlets, either in flagons or on tap, while others sell it under their own proprietary brand. It is available direct from the brewery only by prior arrangement.

ADDRESS
42 Holden Street, Onekawa, Napier
PHONE
(06) 843 3719
FAX
(06) 843 2671
EMAIL
matesbrew@ matesbeer.co.nz
WEBSITE
www.matesbeer.co.nz
BREWERS
Tony Davies & Howard Parkinson

KNIGHTS LAGER

The colour of this beer is best described as mid-straw. The rich aroma has hints of banana, butterscotch and tropical fruit. The texture has improved markedly since last tasting and is now cleaner and crisper

ALCOHOL
4% abv
STYLE
Lager

with a slightly dry back palate. It is lightweight in the New Zealand light-lager style but has plenty of flavour with a reserved hop bitterness that many will find appealing. It is easy drinking and will pair well with hot and spicy food such as barbecued chilli prawns.

MATES AMBER

ALCOHOL	4% abv
STYLE	Amber Lager

Golden-brown with lots of bubbles evident, this beer is light on aroma, with only the merest hint of malt sweetness. It has a very smooth texture, making it easy drinking at low temperature. This is not a highly flavoured beer and is clearly aimed at the Kiwi traditional brown-beer drinker. It will go well with a lamb stew or cottage pie.

MATES DRAUGHT

ALCOHOL	4% abv
STYLE	New Zealand Draught

A slight orange-brown tint gives this beer immediate interest. On the nose it is reminiscent of fruit salad, with a touch of molasses to boot. The texture is clean and very light with no hugely challenging length. It is another typical New Zealand brown beer, low on hops and quite sweet, but with an improved malt influence. Serve it well chilled and this easy-drinking offering will work well as quaffer for the after-match function complete with sausage rolls and a serve of hot chips.

KNIGHTS DARK

ALCOHOL	4% abv
STYLE	Dark Lager

Like many similar beers, this appears black but, held to the light, it is a very dark brown with a firm head. It has a strong burnt-coffee aroma with hints of cooking chocolate. The texture is light — smooth but not creamy — while the flavour is typical caramel and molasses, with a slight bitterness on the very back of the palate. The initial and middle impressions, however, are of sweet iced coffee. Savour it with a bit of wild venison or a pot roast and vegetables.

ROOSTERS BREWHOUSE

ADDRESS
1470 Omahu Road,
Hastings

PHONE
(06) 879 4127

FAX
(06) 879 7410

EMAIL
chris@beachhouse.
co.nz

BREWERS
Chris Harrison &
Shannon Tawhiti

OPEN
Mon–Sat 10 am–
7 pm

Roosters Brewhouse is located on a busy stretch of highway between Napier and Hastings in Hawke's Bay. It's an informal place with a bar and beer garden, and a café serving casual meals. You can sit inside or out and have a refreshing beer or two after a hot day in the Bay.

Roosters is available from the brewery where it is poured through traditional hand pumps, and from select bars in Hawke's Bay and further afield in the lower North Island. The brewery caters mostly to the mainstream taste-buds of local patrons, making batch-brewed beer with no added sugar or preservatives. Every six weeks or so they produce a seasonal or occasional beer — but you may have to ask.

I believe that Roosters beers are developing nicely with some significant improvement in the complexity and balance of the brews. It will be interesting to watch what direction they take in the future.

Over recent times Roosters has produced a Black Cockerel Stout at 6.5% abv and a Best Bitter at 5% abv. I have not had an opportunity to try these beers but their existence is proof positive of the innovation that the guys at Roosters are capable of and the range of styles and flavours to which visitors to their brewery will be exposed.

ROOSTERS LAGER

ALCOHOL
5% abv

STYLE
German-style Lager

This golden lager in the German style has a floral and mild hop aroma infused with a little spiciness/pepperiness. The current version has plenty of flavour and greater hop bitterness. It is still quite sweet but the dryness that carries the experience right to the back palate remains. The texture is smooth and mouth-filling, resulting in a beer that is well balanced and satisfying as an easy-drinking tipple. Choose food that will benefit from this beer's spiciness for maximum enjoyment, perhaps smoked fish pie.

ROOSTERS DRAUGHT

ALCOHOL
4% abv
STYLE
New Zealand
Draught

Its dark gold colour, distinctive aroma of malt fruit, and malty caramel taste place Roosters Draught in the mainstream category — it is made for popular enjoyment and easy drinking. The texture is crisp and clean, with plenty of body and length. There is a touch of citrus to it, particularly orange, and this gives it interest on the back palate. It is well balanced and eminently suitable for drinking in a variety of situations. Understandably popular with locals and visitors to the brewery alike, the brew will be enjoyable with a wide variety of meals — try it with shellfish to accommodate the citrus character.

ROOSTERS DARK ALE

ALCOHOL
5% abv
STYLE
Dark Ale

This beer, to me, has undergone the greatest change since my last tasting of the range. Many aspects of it are familiar — its dark amber-brown colour and wafting roast coffee and liquorice aromas — but the body-weight has improved of late and is much more effective at carrying the flavour. This dark ale has good body and is smooth and easy to drink. Made with a blend of five different malts, it has well-balanced chocolate/coffee flavours with another hint of that liquorice. A slight bitterness marks the finish and makes for pleasant drinking. Enjoy on its own or accompanying roast pheasant or duck or even with a well-made hamburger with generous quantities of meat.

ROOSTERS HAYMAKER LAGER

ALCOHOL
6.5% abv
STYLE
Strong Lager

 TOP BREW

I like the powerful and tasty Roosters Haymaker Lager, which is very pale straw in colour. It has a fruit aroma that brings to mind tinned pineapple as well as other tropical fruit flavours. These notes are supported by a malt sweetness that is carried well by a smooth and mouth-filling texture, and a pleasantly lengthy finish rounds this brew off nicely. The higher alcohol content means it would make a good aperitif; however, you could also serve it with a fruity pudding or a fresh fruit salad.

LIMBURG BREWING COMPANY

Sometimes the local version of a beer in an overseas style is better than the product on which it is based. There are plenty of people who will tell you that Limburg Brewing Company, founded in 1999 and based in Havelock North, makes beers in the German and Belgian style that are easily the equal of their models. Award-winning brewer Chris O'Leary is adamant that only 'best brewing practices, top-quality ingredients and unmatched attention to detail' will deliver beers of the highest quality and character.

I have come to know Chris well through our involvement in BrewNZ. His commitment to his craft and the brewing industry is impressive and he has developed a reputation as a wonderful champion of New Zealand beer. All the Limburg beers are honest representations of the style, some with even greater complexity than their somewhat heartier European cousins. The quality that still impresses me most is their essential drinkability. They are attractively presented, well crafted, full of flavour, refreshing when appropriately chilled and great with food. Distribution has improved dramatically and now Limburg beers are widely available throughout the country as well as from the brewery.

ADDRESS
Havelock Road,
Havelock North,
Hawke's Bay

PHONE
(06) 878 2880

FAX
(06) 878 2771

EMAIL
info@limburg.co.nz

BREWER
Chris O'Leary

OPEN
Tasting Room & Bar
Daily 10 am–4 pm

TOURS
Daily 10 am–4 pm

LIMBURG HOPSMACKER PALE ALE

Hopsmacker is an easy-drinking, well-made draught beer in the pale ale style. It is unfiltered and non-pasteurised and is a soft yellow-gold in colour. Its aroma is one of soft tropical fruit, with some grapefruit and a slightly yeasty touch. English Fuggles and locally grown Saarz hops make their presence felt but never dominate. On the palate it is medium-weight and a blend of fruity, citrusy flavours is evident. The hops kick in again towards the end creating a lovely bittersweet finish. This tasty, refreshing beer will go well with a lemon or orange tart or a fresh green salad.

ALCOHOL
4.5% abv

STYLE
Pale Ale

AWARDS
Silver Medal — Pale Ales, New Zealand Beer Awards 2002
Gold Medal — Pale Ales, New Zealand Beer Awards 2003
Gold Medal — Pale Ales, New Zealand Beer Awards 2004
Trophy — Pale Ales, New Zealand Beer Awards 2004

LIMBURG CZECHMATE PILSENER

The first mouthful of this little stunner nearly knocked my socks off with its incredibly bitter character. But after my palate adjusted I sensed much greater complexity. Some floral and citrus elements made their presence felt and the acetic effect diminished, resulting in a more rounded and balanced finish than first tastes promised. It remains a beer for the hop enthusiast but should not be avoided when tasting the Limburg range, if only for the element of surprise. When choosing a meal partner I would opt for something deep fried, which will benefit from this beer's ability to provide cut-through.

ALCOHOL
5% abv

STYLE
Czech-style Pilsner

 TOP BREW

LIMBURG WITBIER

This golden-brown, cloudy 'white' beer in the Belgian style has an enticing mix of aroma and flavour. It is brewed using malted barley, unmalted wheat and oats, giving it a grainy, musty first impression. This gives way to a fruitier, sweet aroma and the appearance of the additional spices used in the beer — Curaçao orange peel, coriander and a spice that may be cloves. It is thirst quenching when chilled slightly, making it spritzy and slightly tart with a real citrus character. But it becomes truly complex when a bit of warmth encourages vanilla, apple and more aromatic spicy tastes. I would serve it with duck or turkey or perhaps with a fruit steamed pudding and custard.

ALCOHOL
5% abv

STYLE
Belgian-style Wheat Beer

AWARDS
Gold Medal — Wheat Beers, New Zealand Beer Awards 2003

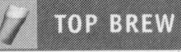 TOP BREW

LIMBURG WEISSBIER

A true-to-style, cloudy wheat beer, this is brewed with German wheat malt and a unique yeast. It has those appealing fruity notes in the aroma and in the taste and the faintest mealy character typical in many wheat beers. The texture is creamy smooth, with enough citrus and banana influences to keep it refreshing. Look for hints of clove as well, although this is not as spicy as some, resulting in much greater balance and encouragement to drink more than a single glass. It will go well with fish, or if you are up for it, I would serve it with traditional trifle.

ALCOHOL
5% abv

STYLE
German-style Wheat Beer

AWARDS
Gold Medal — Wheat Beers, New Zealand Beer Awards 2003

Best in Class — Wheat Beers, New Zealand Beer Awards 2003

 TOP BREW

LIMBURG REDSETTER AMBER ALE

A sparkling red colour makes this an attractive beer in the glass. It is aromatic with hints of malt and some green grass as well. It has good mouth-weight, satisfying rather than heavy, with a sound malt structure underpinning some fruit and hop influences. There is a hint of spice, and as it warms, a little fortified wine character as well. I enjoyed it most as it warmed up when all the different elements seemed to come together and provide a balanced beer likely to have wide appeal. A versatile food beer that will go well with more regular red meat dishes, as well as most game foods.

ALCOHOL
4% abv

STYLE
Amber Ale

AWARDS
Silver Medal —
Amber Ales,
New Zealand Beer
Awards 2003

LIMBURG CYNFUL DARK ALE

Not available for tasting.

ALCOHOL
5% abv

STYLE
Dark Ale

WAITUNA BREWING COMPANY

A very new brewery with a clearly defined and articulated philosophy — to brew beer that uniquely reflects a New Zealand style by using indigenous ingredients. After a few teething problems Bruce and Simon are well underway and with assistance from Nigel Shaw at the Steam Brewing Company in Auckland are producing an attractively packaged beer that has already caught the eye of those responsible for promoting New Zealand products. Taakawa is available from New World supermarkets and selected restaurants and liquor outlets in the North Island, as well as leading tourism operators.

ADDRESS
Rangitikei Valley
Road, Rewa

PHONE
(06) 328 6707

FAX
(06) 632 6707

EMAIL
brewingco@
hotmail.com
waitunabrewingco@
hotmail.com

BREWERS
Bruce Smith and
Simon Burney

TAAKAWA INDIGENOUS ALE

A light gold aromatic beer that shouts 'interesting' from the moment you take the cap from the bottle. It is best described as a light, sweetish lager with a distinctive botanical influence from the addition of native kawakawa leaves that have been substituted for hops. The leaves,

ALCOHOL
5% abv

STYLE
New Zealand
Unhopped Lager

which are hand-harvested immediately before brewing, make their strongest impression at the front and back of the palate, perhaps needing a touch more balance in the middle. The finish is appealing, the brew leaving a warming, satisfying feeling as it goes down. I would serve it chilled with either shellfish or with a smoked chicken salad, although any green salad would partner it well.

SHAMROCK BREWING COMPANY

ADDRESS
92 College Street,
Palmerston North

PHONE
(06) 356 2501

EMAIL
bruce@shamrock.co.nz

OWNER
Bruce McGuigan

BREWER
Daniel Hosking

TOURS
By arrangement

The Shamrock Brewery was established in 1996 by Bruce McGuigan in a pub in the heart of Palmerston North. Today the brewery is located in College Street but the beer is still available at The Shamrock Inn in Main Street, as well as from McGuigan's Restaurant and Bar in Palmerston North.

The brewery operation is managed by Daniel Hosking, the head brewer. Shamrock makes well-established beer styles that are very popular with the regular patrons. Over the years since the first edition of this guide the quality of the beers has improved markedly, with much greater attention now paid to texture and balance. The beers are made in a user-friendly style and continue to be the brand of choice for many locals and also visitors to the city fortunate enough to discover them.

SHAMROCK STRONG BITTER

ALCOHOL
4% abv

STYLE
Dark Lager

This offering, the colour of deep molasses and with a chocolate/caramel aroma, tastes just like roasted coffee beans. It even has the same bitterness on the middle palate. As with many beers, the flavour profile varies greatly depending on the temperature at which the beer is served. At a slightly warmer temperature, Shamrock Strong Bitter has a little sweetness and therefore balance. The texture is crisp and clean and the flavour lasts down the back palate. This beer is best enjoyed at room temperature and with hot roast beef and Yorkshire pudding.

SHAMROCK DARK

A very dark brown, just short of black in colour, this beer has a most interesting aroma best compared with the cowshed at milking time — grassy, warm and rich. The flavour is not so heady, more warm toast in character, with mild maltiness and milder hop. It has less finish than the bitter and is probably a little lighter. Popular with the locals, it will go well with a curry.

ALCOHOL
4% abv
STYLE
New World Black Beer

SHAMROCK DRAUGHT

A rich brown-gold colour makes this an attractive beer in the glass. There is no discernible aroma and the texture is very light. Malt and biscuit-like flavours dominate, making it an easy-to-drink quaffer popular with Shamrock patrons. Enjoy with a pie for lunch.

ALCOHOL
4% abv
STYLE
New Zealand Draught

SHAMROCK STOUT

This is a very dark, almost black beer with a coffee and molasses aroma similar to the bouquet you get when removing the lid from a golden syrup tin. The texture is smooth and clean with improved length. The flavour exhibits coffee and malt-sweetness influences on the front and sides of the palate, with little sign of residual hop bitterness. A pleasant enough beer in the dark-ale style, it will go well with a generous serving of battered shellfish.

ALCOHOL
4% abv
STYLE
Stout

SHAMROCK LAGER

A somewhat darker than expected lager, this beer is straw-gold in colour. It has no aroma to speak of, and a clean rather than crisp finish. The flavour is dominated by a malt sweetness and some fruitiness, with little evidence of hop character to provide that much-needed length. It is a beer style that has many fans and fits easily into the mainstream lager category. This is a palate freshener to take along next time you are invited to a Mexican meal.

ALCOHOL
4% abv
STYLE
Lager

BEER QUOTES 'One of the few moments of happiness a man knows in Australia is that moment of meeting the eyes of another man over the tops of two beer glasses.' **Anonymous, quoted by Bruce Chatwin (1949–89)**

TUI BREWERY (DB BREWERIES)

ADDRESS
Main Road,
Mangatainoka,
Pahiatua

PHONE
(06) 376 7549

FAX
(06) 376 9799

BREWER
Colin Greig

TOURS
Mon–Fri, by
arrangement

Tui Brewery was established at Mangatainoka in the lower North Island in 1889 by entrepreneur Henry Wagstaff. After having a succession of owners, Tui was taken over by DB Breweries in 1969. A massive modernisation programme was undertaken in the following decades and today Tui Brewery is a significant employer in the local community and supports many local events in the region. More than 100 years on, Tui East India Pale Ale is as popular as it was when Henry Wagstaff brewed the beer by hand and delivered it around the district by horse and cart. Tui is easily found from Wellington in the south to Taupo and Whakatane in the north, and it is available at selected retail outlets nationwide. It is now also brewed at Waitemata Brewery, DB's Auckland brewery.

TUI EAST INDIA PALE ALE

ALCOHOL
4% abv

STYLE
India Pale Ale

Over the last few years, 'Tui', as it is commonly known, has moved from being a much-loved regional beer into a nationally recognised brand with its own website, unique marketing proposition involving quirky billboard advertising and wide distribution channels. The flavour profile of the beer has changed little but the sales emphasis it has enjoyed has taken it from a smallish player in the market to one of the biggest associated with sports sponsorship and TV promotion. To describe it as an India Pale Ale is perhaps stretching things a little, it is probably more accurate to say 'in the style of'. It is a medium brown colour and has a malty, chocolate aroma with a hint of caramel as well. The texture is full bodied, smooth and mouth filling, with a short finish. This flavourful beer has a strong malty influence with plenty of residual sweetness and a hint of sweet chocolate in the taste as well. There is little overt hop character but there is some dryness when the beer is enjoyed at room temperature. Tui is a refreshing mainstream match for hearty red meats — beef and lamb, roasts, grills and stews. It will also be an excellent accompaniment for pizza shared with friends.

TUATARA BREWERY

Tuatara has definitely hit its straps since the last edition of this guide when it was still very new. Carl Vasta the brewer continues to bring his considerable energy and expertise to his craft and the range of beers from Tuatara goes from strength to strength. Carl and his partners remain committed to specialising in top-fermented ales and wheat beers. Currently in the line-up are six styles each using their respective traditional brewing ingredients, yeasts and techniques.

The brewery is located at Reikorangi, at the foot of the Akatarawa Range. What drew Carl to the site was the fresh spring water off surrounding hills: 'You cannot make good beer without good water,' says Carl. There are no tasting facilities at the brewery but Tuatara beers are available on tap from two central Wellington outlets — Bodega Bar & Café and the Malthouse — while the packaged beer is available from reputable beer retailers and from Moore Wilson in Wellington.

Note: The tuatara is a reclusive lizard, indigenous to New Zealand and somewhat endangered. The brewery is named after this creature to reflect what Carl and his partners describe as the equally endangered craft of brewing, which demands impeccable ingredients, including appropriate yeasts, as well as plenty of patience.

ADDRESS
138 Akatarawa Road, Waikanae, Paraparaumu

PHONE
(04) 293 3351

MOBILE
027 441 9144

FAX
(04) 293 3051

EMAIL
polarbrewing@clear.net.nz

BREWER
Carl Vasta

TUATARA BOHEMIAN PILSNER

This beer is a pale gold colour and has a strong hop aroma dominated by hop bitterness but with an underlying malt character. It is nicely balanced with good mouth-weight and a lingering finish. It is made with German malt and Czech Saaz hops and, true to style, has a well-balanced taste of fruit sweetness and hop bitterness. It's very drinkable, refreshing and delicious. I would put it with shellfish but it would partner well with any green salad.

ALCOHOL
5% abv

STYLE
Czech-style Pilsner

AWARDS
Gold Medal, BrewNZ New Zealand Beer Awards 2004

 **TOP BREW**

TUATARA INDIA PALE ALE

It's a sparkling gold colour, has a dominant hop aroma with tropical fruit character as well, and is as crisp as they come. It fills the mouth with flavour from English hops, which impart a softly citrus quality. It is refreshing until the last drop with a lingering bitterness capping off a product appreciated especially by hop fans. Serve it with a creamy fettucine and salad, or if you're feeling adventurous, fresh fruit salad.

ALCOHOL
5% abv

STYLE
India Pale Ale

 TOP BREW

TUATARA BELGIAN ALE

An attractive beer in the glass this coppery gold, richly textured beer is made using Saarz hops and light crystal and caramel malts. It is a complex blend of tastes, with the fruity, almost spicy, malt creating the base on which all other elements are balanced. I liked it a lot, especially the way it filled the mouth. It's a complete package with a smooth, lasting finish. Do as the Belgians might and serve it with the best spicy sausages you can find and a creamy potato mash.

ALCOHOL
5% abv

STYLE
Belgian Ale

AWARDS
Silver Medal — Belgian Ales, BrewNZ New Zealand Beer Awards 2004

TUATARA BAVARIAN HEFE

A classic, cloudy wheat beer, with tropical fruit and citrus aromas, medium body-weight and a moderately creamy texture. You will taste tropical fruit and vanilla, malt, yeast and a hint of clove and spice. The overall effect is a bittersweet character on middle palate and at the finish. This beer is well worth seeking out. Any fish or shellfish meal would be ideal for matching.

ALCOHOL
5% abv

STYLE
Unfiltered Wheat Beer

TUATARA ARDENNES STRONG GOLDEN ALE

This high-octane beer is, despite its name, a pale wheat colour. The texture is rich and satisfying, the taste all fruit and spice with the sweet tang of orange making a particular impression. There is plenty of flavour to carry through to the back palate and then the alcohol kicks in. Delicious! A good beer for supping and savouring but if a meal match is essential look for something equally rich, perhaps Szechuan duck.

ALCOHOL
6.5% abv

STYLE
Belgian Strong Ale

AWARDS
Silver Medal — Belgian Ales, BrewNZ New Zealand Beer Awards 2004

 TOP BREW

TUATARA LONDON PORTER

A very good example of the style, this rich porter displays all the characteristics of having been made with quality ingredients. It's aromatic and has nicely balanced malty, fruity, spicy chocolate and caramel tastes from the inclusion of crystal, chocolate and roasted malts. The texture is moderately creamy and carries the flavours well. A touch of spice gives the lingering, bittersweet finish interest. I would consider this well-made beer with a meal of oysters or save it for a chocolate/coffee or caramel mousse at dessert time.

ALCOHOL
5% abv

STYLE
Porter

AWARDS
Silver Medal —
Stouts and Porters,
BrewNZ New
Zealand Beer
Awards 2004

Best in Class —
Stouts and Porters,
BrewNZ New
Zealand Beer
Awards 2004

 TOP BREW

MARTINBOROUGH BEER & ALES

Martinborough Beer & Ales is a newcomer on the New Zealand brewing scene, although brewer Ben Middlemiss has been around for a long time and is well respected. The company is the baby of Rob Harrow and his partner, Fiona Stewart, who have set up the brewery in an old timber mill in the centre of this smallish Wairarapa town.

The town is home to a number of outstanding wineries and gourmet food producers so a craft brewery is a natural addition. Harrow and Stewart are committed to making high-quality craft beers using a combination of traditional and modern brewing techniques. So far things have gone well with critical acceptance of Martinborough beers from both consumers and technical judges at the Australian Beer Awards.

These Martinborough beers are widely available in New World supermarkets, bars and restaurants throughout the Wairarapa and Wellington, as well as from reputable liquor retailers throughout the country.

ADDRESS
Cnr New York and
Princess Streets,
Martinborough

PHONE
(06) 306 8310

MOBILE
0275 245 797

FAX
(06) 306 8320

EMAIL
Fiona.Stewart@
mbc.net.nz

BREWERS
Ben Middlemiss and
Rob Harrow

OPEN
Fri–Sun 12 noon–
7.30 pm, or by
arrangement

MARTINS LAGER

A well-made, European-style lager, yellow-gold in colour, with a decent head, it has a sound malt structure with plenty of hop bitterness on the back palate. A crisp texture and a lengthy aftertaste makes this a better than average thirst quencher. I would match it with seafood, green salad or even a tomato-based pasta to highlight the beer's grassy undertones.

ALCOHOL
5% abv

STYLE
European-style
Pilsner

THE SQUARE ALE

There's plenty of character evident in this tan-colour, slightly cloudy offering. The Maris Otter malt is immediately noticeable in the aroma and the fruitiness it contributes to the taste. The texture is moderately creamy, although it becomes crisper when served chilled. I liked the balance between the malt-generated fruitiness and the impact of the Styrian hops. The overall effect was of a very drinkable and satisfying beer even though it is not as challenging as others in the range. Great with a variety of cuisine but for greatest pleasure I'd go with something tasty and wholesome like steak and kidney pie.

ALCOHOL
5% abv

STYLE
Amber/Golden Ale

AWARDS
Silver Medal,
Australian International Beer
Awards 2004

WHITE ROCK WHEAT BEER

A lovely example of the style. Creamy, soft yellow colour, aromatic with spicy/sweet gentle hints of wheat and citrus, crisp on the palate making it very thirst quenching. Heaps of flavour, with the influence of orange and coriander balancing the impact of the Saaz hop. This beer lasts and lasts with a final burst of tingling spiciness, and an almost brandy-like quality convincing you that the brewers really know the intricacies of the style. I think this beer is the standout of the range and would serve it to begin a meal. For a food match I would go with a tropical fruit salad to leverage off the tastes of orange or, for something more experimental, a Thai chicken salad.

ALCOHOL
5.3% abv

STYLE
Unfiltered
Hefeweizen

AWARDS
Gold Medal,
Specialty Beer
Trophy — Belgian-style Wheat Beer,
Australian International Beer
Awards 2004

 TOP BREW

TORA DARK

If you enjoy Christmas cake, this may be the beer for you. Rich, but with moderate body-weight, it has all the tastes we associate with traditional fruitcakes. Tora is made with an ale yeast and generous amounts of Maris Otter malt. There are touches of caramel, coffee and aromatic allspice in the flavour and it has a smooth texture that coats the mouth in a velvety liquor. An interesting beer that will definitely have its fans, I would serve it with a roast meal, perhaps duck, and with a slice of fruitcake at afternoon tea or for dessert.

ALCOHOL
5% abv

STYLE
Rich Old-style Ale

AWARDS
Bronze Medal,
Australian International Beer Awards 2004

ISLAND BAY BREWING COMPANY

Island Bay Brewing is an anomaly within the boundaries of this guide in that it is not a stand-alone brewery but a marketing company dedicated to providing premium beers to the consumer. The company was established in Wellington in 2002 by supermarket owner, artist and beer lover Maurice Bennett. Maurice is one of those people filled to overflowing with infectious energy and enthusiasm for every project he undertakes. His father was a keen home brewer and Maurice has always loved the stuff, particularly Belgian-style wheat beers. His core business is grocery retailing, specifically the New World supermarket in Island Bay.

A couple of years back Maurice, with a keen eye on the main chance, was exploring ways to liven up his already busy life and, at the same time, was looking to cash in on the success of supermarket beer sales by having his own proprietary brand. He approached a number of brewers who agreed to make beer for him and Maurice has not looked back since. Bennetts beers are now available throughout the lower North Island in bottle form. They will soon be available on tap in select Wellington bars and restaurants.

At the time of writing there were four beers in the range but a 6.5% abv (or higher!) Grand Cru is planned for later in 2005.

ADDRESS
6 Medway Street,
Island Bay,
Wellington

PHONE
(04) 939-8253

FAX
(04) 939-8360

EMAIL
maurice.bennett@
xtra.co.nz

WEBSITE
www.bennettsbeer.
co.nz

BREWERS
Carl Vasta (Tuatara) for the Bennetts Ardenne-style Strong Ale
Paul Cooper (Harringtons, Nelson) for the Bennetts Classic Black and Bennetts 4 Seasons Ale
Mark White (Harringtons, Christchurch) for the Bennetts Wellington Lager

BENNETTS ARDENNE-STYLE STRONG ALE

This beer is brewed by the talented and award-winning brewer Carl Vasta at his brewery set in the hills of northern Wellington. Carl also brews a beer in the same style under his Tuatara brand. The ale is slightly sweet but not cloyingly so; there is a nominal yeastiness as well, all perfectly acceptable in the style. The beer benefits from the obvious addition of extra hops late in the process; the overall impression is of a well-crafted, balanced beer, high in alcohol, double-filtered and very tasty, with a hint of spice at the finish. Very enjoyable, especially when fresh, and poured into a generous-sized glass at the Malthouse in Wellington.

ALCOHOL
6.5% abv

STYLE
Belgian Strong Ale

AWARDS
Silver Medal — Belgium Strong Beer Class, New Zealand Beer Awards, 2003

 TOP BREW

BENNETTS WELLINGTON LAGER

A creamy golden-yellow, this is a much better than average lager. It has body, an acceptable sweetness and a pleasant bitterness, indicating the use of good-quality ingredients, including Nelson hops and malted barley from Canterbury. Brewed to achieve a Belgian beer feel, it has a nicely balanced bittersweet character with a slightly medicinal undertone. It is easy drinking, as well as satisfying, and I recommend serving it with cold meats and fresh breads, gherkins and a mild cheddar.

ALCOHOL
5% abv

STYLE
Premium Lager

BENNETTS 4 SEASONS ALE

The ingredient list on the label of this little number make it sound much more like a meal than a beer! Amazingly, the contribution of each element is in evidence and the result is a complex beer with fascinating layers of flavour. It's not a true ale but rather a lager made with an ale yeast; however, it has good body-weight and texture, an interesting taste and a substantial finish. It is softly golden in colour, with touches of ginger, coriander, honey and vanilla making their presence felt in both aroma and taste. The infusion of elderflowers adds an herbaceous edge. This is the beer for those who prefer less hoppy styles. It is, as the label says, a beer 'for all seasons' and I would serve it with a pork roast and applesauce or even a mild pork curry.

ALCOHOL
5% abv

STYLE
Spice-infused Lager

BENNETTS CLASSIC BLACK

A nice creamy, copper-coloured head introduces this beer, which looks marvellous when poured. Plenty of body, with generous use of toasted and dark malts; well balanced and tasty. This beer is an ideal introduction to the black-beer style; it has all the required characteristics but with a light touch delivering them in easily palatable form. Not just a winter warmer but a year-round beer for a variety of situations. Serve it with rich, red meat dishes or a chocolate dessert with caramel sauce.

ALCOHOL
5% abv

STYLE
Black Lager

AWARDS
Bronze Medal —
Stouts and Porters,
New Zealand Beer
Awards 2004

WELLINGTON BREWING COMPANY

Another Lion Breweries facility, Wellington Brewing Company is a medium-size, state-of-the-art brewery in downtown Wellington, New Zealand's capital city. As well as being a brewery and the headquarters of the company's Wellington sales force, the site is an extremely successful restaurant and bar. A huge glass wall allows a full view of the brewery operations and on brewing day the deliciously mealy smell of simmering malt permeates the building — a perfect reminder that you are in a working brewery.

It has on tap all the beers produced on site, as well as a selection of other Lion products. The beer most often produced is Lion Brown, a regional favourite, but the Wellington Brewing Company at Shed 22 has quickly gained a reputation for producing some of the country's most interesting special brews. Some have become so popular they now make a regular appearance, while others come and go. A favourite feature is the offer to purchase a tasting rack, a series of small glasses of every beer on tap. This is a perfect opportunity to sip and savour, compare the styles and decide on a favourite.

Note: At the time of going to print, Lion Breweries had decided to rebrand all beers produced at Shed 22, except Lion Brown, as

ADDRESS
4 Taranaki Street,
Wellington

PHONE
0800 10 72 72

BREWER
Colin Paige

OPEN
The restaurant and
bar are open Mon–
Fri 11 am–late Sat/
Sun 10.30 am–late
Phone (04) 381
2282

Mac's — Mac's being another Lion company. This will also affect seasonal brews made at Shed 22. The reason for the change is to give the company an option to package these beers for retail sale rather than have them solely in draught form. The beers will continue to be brewed at Shed 22.

WICKED BLONDE

ALCOHOL
4.2% abv

STYLE
All Malt Lager

TOP BREW

My current favourite from the range, this hoppy lager is full of flavour and has a burst of bitterness on the back palate. It is made using a blend of three hop varieties and is both aromatic and flavourful. You will easily discern hints of marmalade and citrus fruit in this beer with its rich, mouth-filling texture. Well chilled, it's very refreshing; at room temperature, it's simply unctuous. I would serve it with mussels steamed open with a dash of Wicked Blonde in the water.

CHEEKY AMARILLO

ALCOHOL
3.7% abv

STYLE
New World Pale Ale

On my last visit I wasn't sure this was quite to my taste. Part of the problem was that it had a flavour note that remained frustratingly elusive. However, I soon determined that the unfamiliar American ale yeast used imparts a complex and interesting favour that you simply cannot ignore. It's fruity and bitter at the same time and as such a real challenge to be savoured and discussed. I'm still not certain that it will be my first choice next visit but I relish the challenge it provided.

SASSY RED

ALCOHOL
4.5% abv

STYLE
Hoppy Best Bitter

The first impression is of an immensely aromatic beer with spice and hop and Christmas fruit indicating there is a complex blend of ingredients. On the palate it's very smooth, making it immediately drinkable. Among the flavours are stewed stone fruit, a mealy character and some fruity esters from the combination of malts. There is plenty of hop influence but it is all nicely in balance. In fact, the popularity of this beer is testament to how the Kiwi palate has quickly found a liking for a higher level of bitterness in their beer. I would serve it with red meat dishes or with an Asian meal where allspice has been used.

LION BROWN

ALCOHOL	4% abv
STYLE	New Zealand Draught

One of the most recognisable of all Kiwi beers, Lion Brown has a provenance all of its own. I am sure the brewers would agree that this is a beer best served well chilled and really fresh, preferably straight from the tap. A rich copper-brown in colour, it has a malty aroma with some moderate hop notes. It is full bodied, almost creamy, with a sweet and nutty taste. It's not a great challenge, rather a good example of a typical Kiwi brown beer for easy drinking with mates in a social environment. Ideal with a rack of lamb or with spare ribs.

VERBODEN VICE

ALCOHOL	5% abv
STYLE	Belgian Cloudy Witbier

An aromatic beer with a pale wheat colour, a generous head and a smooth texture. Banana, Turkish delight and bubblegum notes waft from the glass, while more floral and citrus characters pervade the taste. This is a classic style and it is a very good example of a cloudy witbier with the addition of fresh coriander seeds and Curaçao orange harmonising with raw wheat and Hallertau hops. There is lots going on in this beer and it's well worth taking the time to sip and savour. There is no great bitterness on the end, more a citrus-like tartness, which provides cut-through and adds to its suitability as a food accompaniment. So many foods would match with this, but I would serve either fish to leverage off the citrus, or a lemon-chicken dish where the sweet and sour quality will shine through.

SULTRY DARK

ALCOHOL	4.5% abv
STYLE	Robust Porter

TOP BREW

A deep, deep brown colour, the Sultry Dark is as mysterious as its name suggests. A complex blend of malts produces an aromatic and richly flavoured beer with hints of chocolate and coffee. I also picked up hints of molasses and liquorice, the combination of which gives the beer a distinctly fruitcake character. The texture is substantial, filling every part of the mouth with flavour and providing a lengthy finish. However, don't be misled into thinking this beer may be cloying. The use of Green Bullet and Goldings hops ensures everything remains in balance and its drinkability level stays high. Consider it with venison with rich gravy. It'll be like having two meals in one!

SOUTH ISLAND BREWERIES

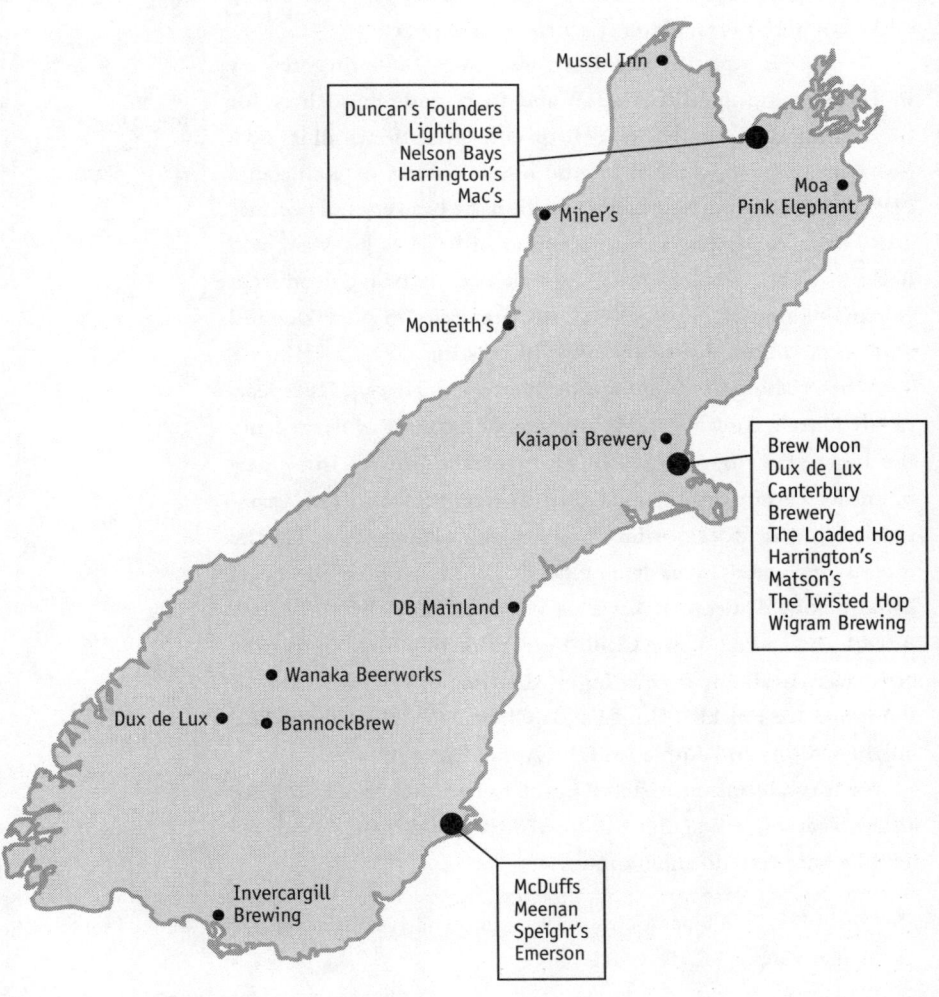

Mussel Inn ●

Duncan's Founders
Lighthouse
Nelson Bays
Harrington's
Mac's

● Miner's

Moa ●
Pink Elephant

Monteith's ●

Kaiapoi Brewery ●

Brew Moon
Dux de Lux
Canterbury
Brewery
The Loaded Hog
Harrington's
Matson's
The Twisted Hop
Wigram Brewing

DB Mainland ●

● Wanaka Beerworks

Dux de Lux ●   ● BannockBrew

McDuffs
Meenan
Speight's
Emerson

Invercargill
● Brewing

MUSSEL INN BUSH CAFÉ

ADDRESS
RD 2, Onekaka

PHONE/FAX
(03) 525 9241

EMAIL
haveabeer@
musselinn.co.nz

WEBSITE
www.musselinn.
co.nz

BREWER
Reuben Lee

OPEN
Daily 11 am–late
Closed for 6 weeks
around August

The Mussel Inn Bush Café is a wonderful discovery halfway between Takaka and Collingwood, in the north of the South Island. Owned by Andrew Dixon, the inn is an unpretentious and friendly place where locals and tourists stop to enjoy good beer and food. The Inn, to the delight of Andrew and his regulars, defies categorisation. One minute it can be a friendly coffee shop and a couple of hours later it's a rip-roaring party.

Andrew, a home brewer from way back, built the brewery in 1995 to indulge his passion and to provide good beer for his customers. Today the busy little enterprise brews all its own beers using pure water from the native forests of Kahurangi National Park. At maximum production the brewery can produce 1200 litres per batch but the number of batches per week will depend on the season and on which beer is being produced. It remains one of the smallest craft breweries in New Zealand and, to my mind, one of the most interesting.

When visiting the Inn, inquire about special brews. Each year, in late March, Andrew and Reuben make a couple of beers using the hops growing around the front of the Mussel Inn — an unknown variety producing a quite different flavour. This variation of flavour does not faze the brewing team, who relish the interest garnered by each new brew. In addition to the beers listed below, Andrew makes Pale Whale Ale 6% abv and Bitter Ass 4% abv and an iconic Chilli Beer, none of which, unfortunately, were available for tasting at the time of my visit. Also in the range are Freckled Frog Feijoa Cider 3–5% abv (depending on the season) and Apple Roughy Apple Cider 4% abv.

No formal tours are offered but if you're interested in having a look around, ask at the bar for Andrew and if he's available he'll be happy to do the honours.

BEER QUOTES 'Prohibition makes you want to cry into your beer and denies you the beer to cry into' Don Marquis (1878–1937)

GOLDEN GOOSE LAGER

ALCOHOL
4% abv

STYLE
Golden Lager

This beer is bright yellow-gold and has a hoppy aroma with some malt sweetness and a lemon/lime aspect. The texture is crisp and clean with good mouth-feel and a pleasant freshness. On the palate the flavours tend towards the sweet end of the spectrum, although there is a slight citrusy bitterness on the back provided mostly by the Saaz hops. With its moderate length, this is a pleasant, easy-drinking beer, and the hop treatment raises its game. It would be good with spicy food — how about home-made chilli meatballs?

DARK HORSE STOUT

ALCOHOL
4% abv

STYLE
Stout

Chocolate-brown, tending towards dark amber, in colour, this beer has an aroma that is full-on coffee beans and fruitcake. It has a good mouth-feel, and the texture is moderately creamy and fresh. The flavour mix is complex, with fruit, chocolate and hazelnut competing for dominance and a strong hop bitterness on the back leaving its mark on the finish. It has plenty of length and may be a touch dry for some. This is a big, robust beer that cries out for similarly robust food — roast beef or lamb shanks is my call.

CAPTAIN COOKER MANUKA BEER

ALCOHOL
4% abv

STYLE
Flavoured Ale

You will either love or hate this brave beer. Writer Keith Stewart in his beer book rated it the only 10/10 beer of all 240 beers he reviewed. Slightly cloudy red-gold in colour, it is highly aromatic, with distinct floral and sarsaparilla (root beer) characters. Some pick up root ginger and/or rose oil flavours as well. It has a creamy texture with lots of length and the flavour is exactly what is promised by the aroma — floral and sarsaparilla-ish — with a hint of citrus. It has the additional interest of being flavoured with manuka tips picked on the day of brewing and added immediately. It is a highly complex beer, full of flavour and promise. It's hard to determine a perfect match but, with its flavour and aroma variety, I would serve it with antipasto.

BEER QUOTES 'They [the British] are like their own beer: froth on top, dregs at bottom, the middle excellent.' **Attributed to Voltaire (1694–1778)**

STRONG OX

ALCOHOL	6% abv
STYLE	Sweet Stout

In the glass Strong Ox is very dark brown with a red tinge. Malt sweetness, caramel and chocolate make up the aroma, while the texture is wonderfully smooth and creamy. The mouth-feel is the great strength of this beer, but the flavour, too, is strong, with a good level of sweetness and bitterness balanced by some chocolate and fruit. Strong Ox is a good supping beer to enjoy with your next roast of game meat — say, wild venison.

WHITE HERON WHEAT BEER

ALCOHOL	4% abv
STYLE	Unfiltered Wheat Beer

Cloudy pale straw is the best way to describe the colour of this offering, which sits somewhere between a hefe and a Kristallweizen. The aroma is citrusy and yeasty, with hints of grapefruit and Juicyfruit chewing gum. The texture is lush and slightly grainy, while the flavour is mildly fruity and floral, with a touch of citrus coming through, especially at the end. White Heron is unfiltered (as are all Mussel Inn beers) but it is a very subtle version with the usual wheat-beer characteristics understated. A short length is another feature, providing a welcome freshness and making it an excellent summer quaffer. It is ideal with fish — grilled hapuku steak with a lemon beurre blanc.

MONKEY PUZZLE

ALCOHOL	10% abv
STYLE	Trappist Red Ale

 TOP BREW

Brewed in the style of a Trappist ale, this bottle-conditioned brew is a rich amber red. A huge aroma of Christmas cake and Marmite hints at what you are about to taste. The body is full — almost a meal — with the equally big flavour dominated by tastes of medicine, malt and fermenting raisins, well carried by the high alcohol content. There is enough residual malt sweetness to sustain the flavour but this is most certainly a supping beer. Rather than risk an inappropriate match, have a big steak meal before you even try this one.

DUNCAN'S FOUNDERS BREWERY

ADDRESS
Founders Historic
Park, 87 Atawhai
Drive, Nelson

PHONE
(03) 548 4638

FAX
(03) 548 4518

EMAIL
founders@
biobrew.co.nz

WEBSITE
www.biobrew.co.nz

OPEN
Daily from 10 am

This 1200-litre brewery became operational early in 1999. It is the first fully organic brewery in Australasia and one of only six in the world. Brewer John Duncan, a fifth-generation Nelson brewer, sources high-quality certified organic ingredients — hops grown in Tapawera near Nelson, pale malt grown and roasted in Canterbury, speciality malts from Germany — and combines traditional brewing techniques and philosophies with the latest technology. The limited size of the local market means that the decision to make fully certified organic beer must be driven by a strong commitment to the values of good health and the protection of the environment rather than any notion of huge sales and great wealth, but the commercial and competition success of John's four organic beers indicates he must be doing something right. In 2002, Founders won the Morton Coutts Trophy for Innovation at BrewNZ for its success in achieving international recognition as a certificated organic brewery producing New Zealand's only fully organic beers.

Founders Brewery is located in Founders Park on the outskirts of Nelson. The park also houses a fascinating working museum that records the history of the district, a family café called The Brewer's Daughter, and a museum of Nelson brewing memorabilia. Duncan's Founders Brewery beers are available at the brewery or in 500-millilitre bottles from good beer retailers.

LONG BLACK

The dark colour and coffee/chocolate aroma of this German-style black beer provide a hint of what to expect in the mouth. John has used plenty of roasted malt to give the beer its cooking-chocolate and cold black coffee characteristics. There is only a low hop influence in both aroma and taste but it is still moderately bitter. The texture is smooth but not creamy and the lasting impression of dryness on the back palate balances out the malt and refreshes the palate. This sup-and-savour beer will partner dark breads and cold meats.

ALCOHOL
4.7% abv

STYLE
German-style
Schwarzbier

AWARDS
Gold Medal,
Australian Inter-
national Brewing
Awards 2002

TALL BLONDE

Made using a blend of four malt varieties and two types of hop, this has a mild aroma of malt and fruit, a crisp, clean body and a generous mouth-feel. It has a quite strong biscuity malt character with attractive fruitiness. It seems to have a more pronounced hop bitterness than my last tasting and I think this adds further to its appeal. This off-dry sweetish beer is easy drinking and is still my pick of the Duncan's Founders brews. Consider serving it with a crisp, green salad.

ALCOHOL
4.7% abv

STYLE
European-style Golden Lager

AWARDS
Silver Medal, Australian International Beer Awards 2002

REDHEAD

A beautiful copper colour in the glass, the Redhead is characterised by a malty aroma and medium body. The taste is a balance of sweet malt and fruit with some roasted malt characters coming through as well. At the back of the palate there is a clean hop bitterness and a slight toastiness that provides a lingering finish. It's an easy-drinking, appealing beer that will go well with food, especially red meat dishes and any with a spicy element.

ALCOHOL
4.7%

STYLE
Vienna-style Amber Lager

AWARDS
Silver Medal, Australian International Beer Awards 2002

GENERATION ALE

A rich tan-brown colour, this new addition to the range is delightful. True to its style, nuttiness is a feature of both its aroma and its taste. The nuttiness underscores the malt and results in a flavour reminiscent of Arrowroot biscuits, long familiar to Kiwis. This flavour combination travels across the palate in a smooth, creamy texture, finishing with a nicely soft hop bitterness on the back palate. This beer will have wide appeal and will partner a range of dishes. I would match it with something that brings out the nuttiness, perhaps roast chicken, a Thai curry with cashews, or even pasta with pesto sauce.

ALCOHOL
4.7% abv

STYLE
Nut-brown Ale

 **TOP BREW**

BEER QUOTES

'The lanky hank of a she in the inn over there
Nearly killed me for asking the loan of a glass of beer;
May the devil grip the whey-faced slut by the hair
And beat bad manners out of her skin for a year.'
James Kenneth Stephens (1882–1950)

LIGHTHOUSE BREWERY

Lighthouse Brewery, named after New Zealand's second-oldest lighthouse, at the entrance to Nelson harbour, has been open since 1996. Friendly owner Dick Tout is a beer fanatic extraordinaire. A keen home brewer and retailer of home-brew products, Dick decided there were ways to take his passion to the masses and opened a brewery in a shop in the heart of Nelson. He has since shifted from there, but Lighthouse remains tiny in comparison with many other craft breweries. Dick brews in batches of 200 litres, making it perhaps the smallest legal brewery in the country. He told me that since moving from his original location he has been able to expand his operations slightly and he is now producing 2–3 brews per week — which has the downside of limiting his time on the golf course!

Dick says his beers are brewed to his own taste, as well as that of his loyal customer base, but I detect a subtle shift towards more challenging styles over the last couple of years. They are available from the brewery in riggers and from local restaurants.

ADDRESS
138B Vanguard Street, Nelson

PHONE
(03) 548 8983

EMAIL
lighthousebrewery@xtra.co.nz

BREWER
Dick Tout

OPEN
Mon–Fri 9.30 am–5.15 pm EXCEPT Tue
Sat 9.30 am–12.30 pm

TASMAN BAY PILSENER

A vibrant mid-gold pilsner-style brew with a light hop and honey aroma, this has a crisp, clean texture both at room temperature and ice cold. The flavour is mild, with a little malt and some hop and citrus character. The beer has good length, especially as it warms, and an overall freshness. It will be good with mussels in sautéed garlic and lemon.

ALCOHOL
4.5% abv

STYLE
New World Pilsner

HAULASHORE BITTER

This mildly perfumed golden offering is initially smooth and creamy, with a fruity malt base and a slightly medicinal mid-palate. There is spice and hop bitterness on the back palate and the finish has a floral sweetness to it. It's very drinkable, especially when chilled down a bit to dull the fairly strident late bitterness that is exaggerated by a crisp ending. I'd save it to wash down a home-made steak and kidney pie.

ALCOHOL
3.6% bitter

STYLE
English-style Bitter

FUG NOSE BPA

A nicely balanced crisp lager style with plenty of hop interest provided by the buckets of Fuggles hops used to brew it. It's aromatic and has good mouth-weight filling the nooks and crannies with grassy, herbaceous flavours and a touch of malt sweetness for balance. There is substantial aftertaste with hop bitterness reminding us of the style. A fascinating drinkable beer with plenty of potential. Shellfish, fish and chips or a platter of antipasto will all partner this brew well.

ALCOHOL
4%

STYLE
British Pale Ale

LIGHTHOUSE DICK'S DARK

Very dark chocolate-brown with a light molasses and Christmas fruit mince aroma. The texture is smooth and fine without being creamy, giving it a crisp mouth-feel. Chocolate comes to mind as flavour; it's almost smoky and medicinal on the back palate. Some bitterness lingers, making it an interesting offering all round. It will be good with food cooked over a flame — grilled steak or even smoked fish.

ALCOHOL
4.5% abv

STYLE
Black Beer

NELSON BAYS BREWERY

Nelson Bays Brewery, known as Bays Brewery, opened in 1993 and is owned by shareholders including hoteliers, beer enthusiasts, engineers and builders. The brewery produces draught beers as a cost-effective alternative to the products of the big breweries. Its main focus is the Nelson Bays area, but product is also available in Blenheim, the West Coast and Wellington, as well as in riggers at the brewery door. Packaged product is available at selected beer retailers and supermarkets around the region.

Look out for their seasonal releases, which have been less widely available. These include the Exclamator Doppelbock (7.5% abv), a full-flavoured favourite brewed using five specialty malts and two hop varieties to produce a distinctive continental-style brew, and the Bengal Bitter Bottle Conditioned India Pale Ale (5.2% abv), a tasty traditional English India Pale Ale. Both of

ADDRESS
89 Pascoe Street,
Stoke, Nelson

PHONE
(03) 547 8097

FAX
(03) 547 8095

EMAIL
mcgrath@ts.co.nz

WEBSITE
www.baysbrewery.co.nz

BREWER
Paul Gibillini

OPEN
Mon–Thu 8 am–
5.30 pm
Fri 8 am–6 pm
Sat 11 am–6 pm
Sun 12.30–5 pm

these were out of season when I last tasted the brews from Nelson Bays, but fortunately for the consumer there are plans to make them permanent additions to the collection. The brewery also produces a traditional dry cider that is well worth trying.

HARLEYS PREMIUM ALE

This beer has quite a history to it, which will undoubtedly be shared with visitors by locals who remember its origins fondly. It is mid-gold in colour and is reasonably aromatic, quite perfumed. In the mouth it is crisp and clean with little overt body-weight. It has a floral, slightly wheaty flavour and a reasonably dry finish. It is a serious alternative for those who like light hop influence and are seeking maximum economy. Thai curry will bring out those floral notes.

ALCOHOL
4% abv

STYLE
Dark Lager

AWARDS
Bronze Medal, Australian International Beer Awards 1998
Bronze Medal, New Zealand International Beer Awards 1999

BAYS GOLD LAGER

Pale straw in colour and with a light hop and malt aroma, this has a crisp and clean texture with a generous mouth-feel and better length than I recall. The flavour tends to the sweetish side of the ledger but is nicely balanced by some citrus characters, specifically lime and orange notes, from the Hallertauer and Saaz hops. It's a sound, unchallenging summer quaffer, best served well chilled, suitable for a barbecue or perhaps chicken satay.

ALCOHOL
4.2% abv

STYLE
Golden Lager

AWARDS
Gold Medal, New Zealand Beer Awards 2003

BAYS DARK ALE

A deep amber hue and a thick, creamy head provide the first impressions of this beer, which uses roast barley rather than roasted malt. The aroma is of molasses and coffee. The texture is lightweight, making it easy to drink, and it has lots of Christmas cake flavours, especially at the front of the palate. A winter warmer, it's one to enjoy as you feast on wonderful Nelson oysters!

ALCOHOL
4% abv

STYLE
Dark Ale

AWARDS
Bronze Medal, Australian International Beer Awards 1995
Bronze Medal, Australian International Beer Awards 1998

BAYS DRAUGHT ALE

This is a standard Kiwi brown beer, resembling golden syrup in colour, with a thick, creamy head when poured. It has a very mild aroma, quite sweet with a touch of honey. The texture is clean and crisp, and the flavour more developed than when previously tried, most likely due to its extended maturation period, with some malt and hop showing through. The finish is sweet and short. A good version of a popular mainstream style, it makes an excellent after-match quaffer to go with hot savouries.

ALCOHOL
4% abv

STYLE
New Zealand Draught

AWARDS
Silver Medal, Australian International Beer Awards 1998

Bronze Medal, Australian International Beer Awards 1999

Bronze Medal, New Zealand International Beer Awards 1999

Bronze Medal, New Zealand International Beer Awards 2000

Bronze Medal, New Zealand International Beer Awards 2002

HARRINGTON'S BREWERY NELSON

Harrington's Brewery in Nelson is an offshoot of its parent brewery in Christchurch. Craig, the Nelson brewer, is the son of John, who owns Harrington's in Christchurch. Craig opened the Nelson operation in 1997 with a view to sharing Harrington's beers with patrons in the upper South Island. Some of the beers brewed in Christchurch — the Draught, Big John and Heritage Dark (see pages 125–129) — are also available in Nelson. At the same time Craig, who is passionate about his hops, brews additional beers, of which the Wheat Beer and the Stout are available at Harrington's in Christchurch. At the moment the Nelson range is available in flagons directly from the brewery, on tap from the Builder's Arms in Blenheim and in draught

ADDRESS
53 Beach Road, Richmond, Nelson

PHONE/FAX
(03) 544 8675

BREWERS
Craig Harrington & Paul Cooper

EMAIL
craig@ harringtonsbrewery.co.nz

WEBSITE
www.harringtonsbrewery. co.nz

OPEN
Mon–Wed 10 am–6 pm
Sat 10 am–7 pm

form from Harrington's Bottle Shop in Tahunanui. The Boulder Bank range is available in packaged form from selected outlets. You might also like to try the Harrington's Cider and Harrington's Scrumpy made in the English style at the brewery.

HARRINGTON'S BEST BITTER

The dark copper colour of this offering looks good in the glass, while the distinct aroma of peaches and pears with clear evidence of hops is immediately appealing. In the mouth it is rich and mouth-filling, has plenty of body and is full of flavour. The taste is of malt and caramel with a good level of hop bitterness and some welcome dryness on the back palate. Choose full-flavoured meat dishes to go with this beer — black-pepper steak comes to mind.

ALCOHOL
5% abv
STYLE
Copper Lager

HARRINGTON'S FINEST LAGER

Pale to mid-straw in colour, this beer has a fairly strong aroma heavy with cut grass and tropical fruit influences. The texture is clean with a little stickiness, and on the back palate it is slightly dry. It is light on flavour in the New Zealand light-lager style and has only moderate hop bitterness, which many will find appealing. Easy drinking, it will pair well with hot and spicy food, as well as salami on rye.

ALCOHOL
5% abv
STYLE
Pilsner

HARRINGTON'S WHEAT BEER

Pale yellow-gold with a light, distinctively white head and a low level of carbonation, this beer has an aroma of milled grain and a medium malt-fruit sweetness. It is well balanced in texture, with good mouth-feel and a light hop bitterness. The flavour is mild and slightly dusty, with evidence of fruit and the wheat. This is a beer with a certain appeal, well made and likely to partner herbaceous and sweeter food well. I would serve it with sweet and sour fish, or something similar.

ALCOHOL
5% abv
STYLE
Wheat Beer

HARRINGTON'S STOUT

As you would expect, this one is very dark brown in colour, with a slight amber hue. The aroma is full, with lots of chocolate and toffee character and a touch of caramel. As it warms there is a smoky, burnt-

ALCOHOL
5% abv
STYLE
Stout

coffee influence. The mouth-feel is smooth and a little creamy with plenty of length. Sweeter coffee and Christmas fruit mince flavours dominate the palate, giving it porter-like characteristics. A mainstream example of the style, lightweight with good length, it will go well with a hot smoked-beef sandwich.

HARRINGTON'S TASMAN LAGER

ALCOHOL
6.5% abv

STYLE
Strong Lager

The recipe for this beer has changed markedly since I first reviewed it, and for the better I might add. It is still a full-strength lager with a hell of a kick, but it is well balanced and very good. The aroma is quite subtle, with a bit of hop making its mark. The texture is clean and crisp, the mouth-feel full and satisfying. On the palate it has plenty of bite, some sweetness and lots of hop influence. There is ample length, with moderate hop bitterness and a pleasant dry character. A flavourful lager, it will go best with equally loud food. Just for fun, try it with your favourite hamburger from the local takeaway or, if you seek something more sedate, a strong liver pâté!

HARRINGTON'S CANTERBURY PALE ALE

ALCOHOL
5% abv

STYLE
American-style Pale
Ale

This American-style pale ale is mid-tan in colour and has a sweet honey-and-fruit aroma with some hoppiness. The texture is crisp and fresh, leaving an impression of balance with good mouth-feel. The flavour is very hoppy from start to finish. The hops also impart their characteristic bitterness, giving the beer good length and a pleasant dryness — creating an appeal for more. If hop influence is your preference, here is a beer sure to please. It will go well with any dishes that have a herbaceous element — enjoy it with a tomato-based pasta dish or roast chicken and salad.

BOULDER BANK LAGER

ALCOHOL
4% abv

STYLE
Lager

This is a lightweight quaffing lager with a strong malt and hop aroma and a clean, easy-drinking texture. I found the flavour a bit tart and citrusy, but the beer is well made for the average Kiwi palate. It will partner any spicy food well, or you may like to serve it with shellfish.

BOULDER BANK DRAUGHT

With about the same level of complexity as Boulder Bank lager, this draught has an aroma of malt, with some toffee and banana influences. There is also a faint suggestion of mealiness. The texture is light, while the flavour is moderately fruity. It is dry around the palate with some citrus character towards the back. It finishes early but will match well with food. Try it with lasagne.

ALCOHOL
4% abv

STYLE
New Zealand Draught

BOULDER BANK DARK

Continuing in the same vein as its easy-drinking cousins, this dark is moderately flavoured but very light in texture. It has traces of the expected chocolate and caramel characters, as well as a strongly medicinal finish. There is more length to the Dark but the overall effect is of an uncomplicated beer for the mass market. Beef stew and kumara mash is my pick for partnership.

ALCOHOL
4% abv

STYLE
Dark Lager

MAC'S BREWERY

The Mac's range of all-malt ales and lagers is batch-brewed at Mac's, formerly McCashin's Brewery & Malthouse, established by South Island farmer and publican Terry McCashin in 1981 in an old cider brewery in Stoke, Nelson. McCashin's was considered by some to be the first commercial microbrewery to offer any serious competition to Lion and DB. However, from the outset the brewery produced a different style of beer. Its brewing philosophy determined that Mac's beer products adhered to the Reinheitsgebot, the Bavarian beer purity law of 1516, which countenances no use of chemicals, preservatives, artificial colourings or other adjuncts. Without doubt this positioning attracted many customers earlier in the company's development.

In 1999 Lion purchased the brand and then in 2000 began leasing the brewery, which is still owned by Terry McCashin. Lion has certainly given the brand wider distribution and profile

ADDRESS
660 Main Road, Stoke, Nelson

PHONE
(03) 547 5357

FAX
(03) 547 6876

WEBSITE
www.macs.co.nz

TOURS
Daily 11.15 am & 2 pm (summer)
Daily 11.15 am (autumn/winter)

and brought further sophistication to brewing methods.

Apart from the standard range, which is available nationwide in draught and packaged form, as well as online from the Mac's website, Mac's has produced some very successful seasonal beers. These include Blonde Mac, AroMac, which used the locally developed hop cultivar Nelson Sauvin, and my favourite Peated Malt Mac, a wonderfully full-flavoured beer with strong peat, whisky and smoky flavours. It is not certain if these beers will be produced again, but ask for them at the bottle stores anyway — you may be in luck.

MAC'S GOLD

Undoubtedly the most famous of all the Mac's products, the Gold is, in fact, light-straw in colour and carries a substantial, creamy head. Fruit and hops are present in the aroma, with suggestions of citrus and honey as well. The texture is light and clean with moderate mouth-feel. Subtle is the best way to describe the flavour: the malt comes through and there is some mild bitterness towards the end, as well as a suggestion of citrus and yeastiness. The finish, while short, is refreshing. For a food match I would suggest roast chicken with well-herbed stuffing.

ALCOHOL
4% abv

STYLE
Golden Lager

AWARDS
Bronze Medal — New Zealand Golden Lager, New Zealand Beer Awards 2004
Silver Medal — New Zealand Golden Lager, New Zealand Beer Awards 2003
Gold Medal — Australian-style Lager, Australian International Beer Awards 2002

MAC'S LIGHT

It's not easy to make a light beer that has full flavour and the characters of a regular-strength beer. Mac's Light, however, is a reasonably good example. Pale straw in colour with a moderately bitter aroma of grain and grass, it has a texture that is mildly creamy and a mouth-feel that is quite lightweight. The flavour is fairly hoppy, although there is a moderate level of sweetness as well. This beer has an early finish but is pleasant and refreshing enough. Many foods will dominate, so subtlety is the key. I'd go for white fish poached in white wine and seasoned with freshly ground pepper.

ALCOHOL
1% abv

STYLE
Low-strength Lager

MAC'S RESERVE

Previously branded as Mac's Nelson Reserve this rendition is mid-straw in colour, with a creamy, white head. It has a very mild aroma, with only the most subtle malt notes showing through. The texture is rich and creamy with plenty of mouth-feel, while the flavour is sweet and spicy, malty with strong caramel and some yeasty influences as well. There is a pleasant, moderate-level hop bitterness that comes through at the end and finishes off this crisp brew nicely. Even though this, too, underwent some tweaking in 2003, it remains my favourite in the Mac's standard range. Mac's Reserve is an interesting beer that will appeal to those looking for something to sup and savour. Try it with creamy chicken fettucine or a peppered steak.

ALCOHOL
5.2% abv

STYLE
European-style Lager

AWARDS
Gold Medal, Best in Class — New Zealand Premium Lager, New Zealand Beer Awards 2004
Gold Medal — European-style Lager, Australian International Beer Awards 2004

 **TOP BREW**

MAC'S BLACK

A deliciously dark brown colour marks what was formerly known as Black Mac, which ranks as one of the first 'dark' beers — at least in modern times — to strike the palate of the Kiwi beer drinker. It underwent a style revision in 2003, but its essential characteristics remain the same, if somewhat better defined. Its aroma is of Christmas cake and floral malt, while the texture is rich and smooth and moderately creamy, making it a good beer to drink through the head. Gentle flavours of malt, liquorice and caramel emerge and I also detected some pleasant nuttiness. There is good length and a malt sweetness to the finish. Enjoy this with Nelson oysters.

ALCOHOL
5% abv

STYLE
German-style Schwarzbier

AWARDS
Bronze Medal — German-style Schwarzbier, New Zealand Beer Awards 2004
Silver Medal — German-style Schwarzbier, Australian International Beer Awards 2004

MAC'S BLONDE

A European-style brew that proved very popular with Kiwi drinkers when launched as a seasonal offering in 2000, Blonde Mac is a refreshing light lager with a complex and interesting flavour profile. It is brewed using a proportion of wheat and during maturation it is infused with orange peel and freshly ground coriander. As a result it has a fruit and spice taste with a lovely citrus overtone. The texture is crisp and clean and the end result is a tasty palate cleanser. This is a

ALCOHOL
5% abv

STYLE
Spice-infused Lager

AWARDS
Silver Medal — Herb and Spice Beers, Australian International Beer Awards 2002

very drinkable brew in its own right but also goes well with food. Try it either with gently pan-fried fresh fish fillets and a squeeze of lemon or lime or with cold chicken and watercress salad.

MAC'S COPPERHOP

Born of the need for a Limited Release beer for the Festive Brew Section at BrewNZ in 2002, the Copperhop India Pale Ale went on to win a Gold Medal in the Pale Ale section of the New Zealand Beer Awards, further enhancing its success with a Best In Class. Subsequently, Copperhop has become a permanent member of the Mac's range. It's another favourite of mine and has a wonderful fruity-spice aroma that offers up hints of exotic fruit such as gooseberry, grapefruit and passionfruit. It has a pleasantly hoppy character and a welcome bitterness offsetting the sweetness of fruit and malt. A well-constructed body makes this a very enjoyable tipple indeed. I would opt for the best steak money can buy, gently grilled and served with jacket potatoes and lashings of butter.

ALCOHOL
5% abv

STYLE
New World Pale Ale

AWARDS
Gold Medal, Best in Class — Pale Ales, New Zealand Beer Awards 2002

Silver Medal — India Pale Ale, Australian International Beer Awards 2002

Bronze Medal — India Pale Ale, Australian International Beer Awards 2003

Silver Medal — American Pale Ale, Australian International Beer Awards 2004

 TOP BREW

MOA BREWING COMPANY

The Moa Brewing Company was established in 2003 by Josh Scott, a young man from a family with an enviable wine pedigree. Currently, only one beer is being produced by a contract brewery in Blenheim, although Josh plans to have his own brewery up and running in the very near future. In addition to classic brewing processes Josh and his brewer Graham Mahy have employed wine-making techniques to give Moa a strong point of difference. It is bottled, fermented and conditioned to give a natural, consistent carbonation. The beer is left to lie on its lees for around six

ADDRESS
Jacksons Road, RD 3, Blenheim, Marlborough

PHONE
021 502 707

EMAIL
josh@alanscott.com

BREWER
Graham Mahy

weeks before it is bottled and topped up with a little more yeast and sugar. It then ferments for a second time, a process that takes two to three weeks before being 'disgorged', which involves removing most of the sediment from the bottle and which distinguishes wines made in the Methode Traditionelle style. The beer is then quickly topped and a cork and musslet (wire cage) are promptly put onto the bottle. The bottle is then washed, dressed with labels and packaged ready for sale.

MOA METHODE TRADITIONELLE

ALCOHOL	5.5% abv
STYLE	Bottle-fermented Lager

Moa is well made with a solid malt base and an abundance of hoppy notes that give the impression of sweet fruit, grassy overtones and a balanced astringency that is complex and pleasing to the nose. The palate is fruity with a little spiciness and a balanced hop flower bitterness that has a very long-lasting finish. It is well carbonated and this adds to its sense of freshness. This beer will be enjoyable with many foods from big game to pasta dishes or equally as a sup-and-savour brew all on its own.

PINK ELEPHANT BREWERY

ADDRESS	Rapaura Road, Renwick, Marlborough
PHONE/FAX	(03) 572 9467
EMAIL	pinkelephantbrewery@ paradise.net.nz
BREWER	Roger Pink

Open since December 1990, the colourfully named Pink Elephant Brewery is owned by the equally colourful Roger Pink. Roger is an Englishman who has set out to mimic the beer styles of his homeland, and he spares no effort in reproducing exactly the right conditions. Roger produces his own special malts and uses Nelson hops to produce top-fermented, naturally conditioned ales of intricate flavour and aroma for the real English-style beer aficionado.

Since the last edition of this guide, Roger has reduced the number of beers he regularly brews, opting instead to stick to a favoured few, supplemented when the fancy takes him with special seasonal offerings.

Unfortunately, there's no public access to the brewery so you will have seek out Roger's beers in better liquor retailers around the country, including Regional Wines and Spirits in Wellington and Hamilton Wines and Spirits in Hamilton. Alternatively, all Pink Elephant products can be purchased by mail order. I rate Pink Elephant beers and Roger Pink very highly. They can be quite challenging but if you are looking for some fascinating brews it's well worth making the effort to seek them out.

MAMMOTH

The quirkily named Mammoth is a dark amber-red, aromatic with distinctive rich fruit and soft malt characters. The texture is rich and creamy, filling the mouth with luscious, malty flavours and some dark fruit (dates and raisins), together with firm hop bitterness. These flavours linger long and strong, providing a wonderfully true ale with mammoth-sized flavour. The high alcohol content makes this an excellent aperitif and an equally good digestive if simply served with a traditional ploughman's lunch or a rich rabbit stew.

ALCOHOL
7% abv

STYLE
Amber Ale

 TOP BREW

GOLDEN TUSK

Another full-strength top-fermented ale, Golden Tusk (originally named PBA) is an English-style special bitter. It is a rich golden yellow in the glass and the aroma is hoppy with some caramel and a floral character coming through as well. In the mouth it is creamy and has the freshness that characterises all of the Pink Elephant beers. The flavour is full, with enticing residual hoppiness, some toffee sweetness to maintain balance and a special garden-herb character as well. There is enough hop bitterness to satisfy the hop-heads and plenty of length for the rest of us. This is a lovely food beer to enjoy with a range of dishes: just for fun try it with fish and chips — without the vinegar!

ALCOHOL
4% abv

STYLE
English-style Bitter

 TOP BREW

RAJAH

This beer is brewed in the style of an 'old' ale and is very dark, almost black. The creamy, clinging head is impressive, as is its aroma of complex roasted malt and toffee. In the mouth it is robust and satisfying with tastes of roasted malt and a lingering bitter liquorice finish. There is enough sweetness to provide balance and it finishes with a flavour-filled flourish. Have this one as a late-night tipple or serve it with a hearty roast and three vegetables. Try using a little in the gravy just for a change.

ALCOHOL
5.5% abv

STYLE
Old Ale

 TOP BREW

ROGERS RESERVE

Described as a pale ale, this beer is dark gold to amber in colour with a fine white bead hinting at its creamy texture. It has definite berryfruit characters on the nose — mostly strawberry. The flavour is a combination of malt, fruit and hops and it finishes with an attractive hop bitterness that carries the flavour to the last. A very pleasant drink, try it with roast chicken or a creamy pasta dish — say, fettucine.

ALCOHOL
6% abv

STYLE
Pale Ale

 TOP BREW

MINER'S BREWERY

Originally owned by four local hoteliers, Miner's Brewery in the small West Coast town of Buller is still locally owned and operated with majority shareholders Alan and Jo Absalom firmly in charge. Support for the brewery from the 5000-strong local population is fervent; demand for Miner's brews is so strong that the beer is still delivered by the tanker-full, making Miner's one of the few craft breweries still distributing this way. If success is measured by market share in the local area, Miner's Brewery must hold some sort of record for its influence in Buller and the West Coast region. The beers are brewed unashamedly to satisfy local taste buds, but there is plenty of interest for the visiting beer drinker. The range is available both from the brewery and on tap at many West Coast pubs. Alan Absalom and his team also brew Green

ADDRESS
10 Lyndhurst Street, Westport

PHONE/FAX
(03) 789 6201

EMAIL
absalom@xtra.co.nz

WEBSITE
www.greenfern.co.nz

BREWER
Dean Lamplough

OPEN
Mon–Fri 8.30 am–5.30 pm
Sat 11 am–5.30 pm

Fern Lager, an organic beer marketed under the name Green Fern Brewery to emphasise that key production facilities comply with requirements for organic certification.

BARRACUDA PILSNER

ALCOHOL
4% abv
STYLE
All Malt Lager

Sometimes labelled Miner's Gold, this lager-style all-malt beer is pale straw in colour but in the right light could be called gold. There is a definite hop character on the nose and the texture is exactly as it should be: light and refreshing. I detected a slight graininess that added a certain character to a mainstream product. The flavour suggests honey with the hop coming through again, and while the beer is sweet there is no lingering cloying character. In the middle there is some biscuit character, while a good level of hop bitterness provided by the Saaz hops is present on the back palate. This is a good session beer, especially with whitebait fritters!

MINER'S DRAUGHT

ALCOHOL
4% abv
STYLE
New Zealand Draught

The colour is copper-gold, and the aroma is of malty sweetness with fruit mince and caramel. The texture is quite busy and the beer seems highly carbonated, making it a refreshing drink at any time of the year. On the palate the taste is malty rather than hoppy, although there is a little bitterness towards the back. It has a short finish and some residual sweetness. This is a good quaffer in the nature of a Kiwi brown beer, and has a bit of class that takes it above the average for this style. It will go well with most red meat dishes — I'd serve it with venison steaks.

MINER'S DARK

ALCOHOL
4% abv
STYLE
New Zealand Black Beer

A nice, dark chocolate in colour with a red tinge to it, this beer has an aroma that also brings to mind chocolate — with a bit of caramel/ toffee thrown in for interest. The texture is crisp and clean, and the flavour has lots of depth but not much length. On the palate it tastes like cold coffee and chocolate, with a malt fruitiness adding some sweetness. It has plenty of flavour on the middle palate and is akin to a porter in style, but there is little hop interest for hop-heads or body to carry the flavour through to the finish. If seeking a meal match, save it for the Sunday roast.

GREEN FERN LAGER

ALCOHOL
5% abv

STYLE
Organic Lager

This wholly organic, broadly international-style lager has the all-important official Bio-Gro certification. Made without cane sugar, preservatives or flavourings, Green Fern has a fresh, hoppy and floral aroma. It is clean and crisp on the palate with a lively hop influence provided by the organic Pacific Gem hops used. The taste is a well-balanced mix of malt and hop and there is plenty of length to the finish. This is the organic flagship of the company and is exported to Australia and Japan. A very pleasant beer that will go extremely well with chicken and pasta, it is available in most supermarkets.

MONTEITH'S BREWING COMPANY (DB BREWERIES)

ADDRESS
60 Herbert Street, Greymouth

PHONE
(03) 768 4149

FAX
(03) 768 6604

EMAIL
info@monteiths.co.nz

WEBSITE
www.monteiths.co.nz

HEAD BREWER
Barrie Calder

TOURS
Mon–Fri 10 am, 11.30 am & 2 pm
Sat–Sun 11 am & 2 pm
Cost $10, children free

I have come to know the beers from Monteith's Brewing Company very well over the last eight years. Over that time I have been the independent convenor of judging for the Monteith's Wild Food Challenge, an annual competition that has restaurants, cafés and bars around the country competing to find which is the most expert at matching the aromas, textures and tastes of Monteith's products with game food. It is amazing how much better the entries have become. They are more sophisticated, more complex and more successful each year.

It is fair to say that as a brand Monteith's still has the high ground on beer and food matching, although it may have relinquished a little territory in the area of seasonal beers. Where it was once the undisputed leader it is now only one of a number of players.

The company has been a proud West Coast brewer since 1858, and has been producing Monteith's Original Ale in one guise or another since the coast was in the grip of gold fever well over a century ago. Today, Monteith's beers are brewed at the company's main brewery in Waitemata, Auckland, as well as at the original Greymouth site, where an illustrious tradition continues with beer that is batch-brewed in 12,000–19,000 hectolitre lots, using coal-fired boilers, open fermenters, natural ingredients and fresh water from the region. All the Monteith's brands are made using New Zealand hops; all are microfiltered.

Periodically, the company releases a seasonal offering for sale over a short term and these tend to be beers with plenty of flavour and interest, although some less challenging offerings sometimes emerge.

The most successful of these is Summer Ale, which regularly sells out over the summer period, despite increased production each year. The range, available throughout the country in attractive 350-millilitre bottles, is garnering a lot of interest, especially among dedicated beer lovers.

MONTEITH'S ORIGINAL ALE

A favourite with West Coasters, this golden-brown classic beer in the Kiwi brown-beer style is especially enjoyable when served from the tap in the company of Greymouth locals. Its full, malty aroma, crisp, clean texture and plenty of mouth-feel is satisfying and the moderate level of hop influence, especially towards the end keeps it clean. The taste flavour remains reasonably sweet but both malt and hop show their independence. I detected a little more toffee character this time around and an attractive off-dry quality in the draught version probably due to its freshness. The beer, which started life based on an English ale, has good length and a short and pleasant aftertaste. The brewers recommend serving this with whitebait but I'd probably go for something a bit more weighty — perhaps mussels with a drizzle of oil and balsamic grilled in the half shell and served with bread or even a traditional beef or lamb hot pot.

ALCOHOL
4% abv

STYLE
New Zealand
Draught

TOP BREW

BEER FACTS The Sumerians drank their beer through straws that were hollow stalks of corn.

MONTEITH'S GOLDEN LAGER

ALCOHOL	5% abv
STYLE	Golden Lager

This easy-drinking beer is the biggest seller in the portfolio, and while well made, possibly the least interesting. It's a straw-coloured lager with a hint of green to it. The aroma is mild with the hop character sitting nicely in the background. The texture is lightweight, clean and crisp especially when chilled right down. It has a sweetish full flavour, rich and malty with a slightly nutty character balanced by a hint of yeastiness and mown grass. There is also a hint of almond/marzipan on the sides of the palate. The mouth-feel and length are both generous for the style and the aftertaste demonstrates both sweetness and dryness, keeping the beer refreshing. I would go with a salmon dish — perhaps with a moderate serving of a creamy dill mayonnaise. Alternatively, a mild Thai curry will bring out the fruitiness in the beer nicely.

MONTEITH'S CELTIC RED BEER

ALCOHOL	4.4% abv
STYLE	Celtic Red Beer

This is named more for its characteristic sparkling red-tan colour than its fidelity to any particular Irish beer style. It's interesting to note that there is chocolate malt in this beer which, rather than giving it any significant chocolate taste, seems to accentuate the maltiness of both the aroma and the taste. It has a crisp texture, while the flavour is full of soft fruitiness. The delightfully crisp, short, dry finish carries gentle roasted notes through to the aftertaste. A well-rounded, smooth brew, with plenty of cut-through to keep the palate awake. It is also a beer for the traditionalists, who will enjoy its uncomplicated, generous character. Any red meat roast — especially served with mushrooms — will partner this beer well, but in the spirit of the wild West Coast I'd have venison or spit-roasted hogget.

MONTEITH'S PILSNER BEER

ALCOHOL	5% abv
STYLE	Czech-style Pilsner

Pale gold in colour, this Czech-style beer is mildly aromatic with a hint of cut grass and hay, with some melon influence as well. The mouth-feel is full and generous, while the texture is crisp and clean. The flavour is complex, with herbal and well-defined citrus hop characters from the Saaz hops and some spiciness together with a hint of grapefruit providing the interest. There is residual sweetness from the combination of crystal and pale malt and a pleasant dryness giving a clean and lingering aftertaste. This is a beer that the hop-heads appreciate. For a stylish twosome, try it with crayfish.

MONTEITH'S BLACK BEER

ALCOHOL
5.2% abv

STYLE
New Zealand Black
Beer

This excellent example of the dark beer style is finding lots of followers. It is a deep dark brown colour and has a rich aroma full of malt with some roasted malt and chocolate notes as well. The texture is equally rich, although lighter in body and less creamy than you might expect. It has great mouth-feel, smooth and delicate, and the flavour is of coffee and roasted chocolate — with just enough hop dryness to provide a bittersweet balance to the chocolate/malt character. Don't shy away from making this an all-year-round option. In warmer months it will stand a slight chilling. This beer is perfect with smoked eel or, if you have the calling, raw oysters.

MONTEITH'S RADLER

ALCOHOL
5% abv

STYLE
Belgian Flavoured
Ale

The newest permanent addition to the Monteith's family, Radler (after the Flemish word for cyclist), is a concept that was years in the making and was first released as a seasonal beer. I prefer it to the sweeter Summer Ale. It has a sweet lemon aroma and a spritzy, mouth-filling texture. Nicely balanced, some hop bitterness but a more extensive citrus character. This easy-drinking beer is ideal for warmer months or as an après-sport refresher. Alternatively, any fresh shellfish or fish dish, especially those with a bit of spice, will benefit from the dominant lime character in this beer.

MONTEITH'S SUMMER ALE

ALCOHOL
5% abv

STYLE
Flavoured Lager

A regular seasonal beer in the Monteith's range, Summer Ale has a very soft straw colour. It has a powerful aroma of ginger and spice with some maltiness evident, too. The texture is really crisp and this beer should be enjoyed ice cold to maximise the effect of the texture. It has good mouth-feel and a full flavour of malt, ginger and spice with some tropical melon flavours. It's reasonably sweet but with a refreshing dryness towards the end. You might try a wedge of orange or lime with this delightful seasonal offering. My suggestion for a meal match is cold wild pork and salad, but I'd also serve it to lunch guests with an orange sherbet.

KAIAPOI BREWERY

Unpretentious and laid back in its approach to brewing under the control of Kerry Neville, Kaiapoi Brewery provides two beers, mainly for local consumption. They are not brews for the beer fanatic; rather, they are uncomplicated quaffers, batch-brewed without added sugar — basic beers for the ordinary consumer. Having supplied local outlets such as the Kaiapoi Crossing Bar and Kaiapoi Liquor Centre for many years, Kaiapoi also sells its products in draught and 330-millilitre bottles at its brewery at the Southern Grain Spirits plant in Kaiapoi, as well as selected privately owned bars and hotels in and around Christchurch.

ADDRESS
Southern Grain Spirits (NZ) Ltd, 9a Peraki Street, Kaiapoi

PHONE
(03) 327 6389

FAX
(03) 327 6233

EMAIL
sgrainpromo @xtra.co.nz

WEBSITE
www.southerngrain. co.nz

BREWER
Kerry Neville

OPEN
Mon–Thu 9 am– 5.30 pm
Fri 9 am–6 pm
Sat 10 am–6 pm

TOURS
By appointment

FINNEGANS TRADITIONAL DARK ALE

This beer combines the positive characteristics of earlier brews with added weight and a more balanced finish. It has a dark molasses colour from the coloured malts and a strong malt aroma with hints of coffee and caramel. It is medium in body with tastes of toasted malt and molasses with a touch of burnt coffee. It is still quite bitter on the finish, but is more rounded and with a touch of sweetness. For a food match I would choose pork with applesauce.

ALCOHOL
4% abv

STYLE
Full Malt Lager

KAIAPOI DRAUGHT

An assertive, grassy, citrus aroma still introduces this red-copper beer. The texture is lightly weighted and the flavour repeats the green grass and citrus notes, more familiar in some lagers than in a typical Kiwi draught. It has a well-defined bitterness on the back palate. I would like to see some additional richness to keep this fully in balance, perhaps the addition of extra malt? It is a big improvement on previous versions and remains a satisfactory quaffing beer enjoyed by locals used to Kaiapoi's distinctive style of brew. This is another option to complement a grilled meat dish.

ALCOHOL
4% abv

STYLE
New Zealand Draught

BREW MOON BREWING COMPANY

Unlike most breweries whose roots lie in the traditional brewing areas of Belgium, Germany and England, The Brew Moon Brewing Company was born of a seed planted in Northern California. Owners Kieran McCauley and Belinda Gould, at the time living in San Benito County, were smitten by the style of beer being produced by the many microbreweries around San Francisco and to the north in Oregon and Washington. After three years of enjoying handcrafted hoppy beers, they returned to North Canterbury in 2001 to find a flagging café with a dilapidated cider-making facility attached. They completed the much-needed renovations and created The Brew Moon Brewery and Café, opening in July 2002.

ADDRESS
150 Ashworth's Road (SH 1) Amberley, Christchurch

PHONE
(03) 314 8036

FAX
(03) 314 8136

EMAIL
mcgould@ihug.co.nz

BREWER
Carl Hadler

OPEN
Wed–Sun From 11am

Initially serving brews from other small producers from throughout the South Island, Brew Moon produced its first Amberley Pale Ale in February 2003. Soon to follow were its Broomfield Brown Ale, Dark Side Stout and more recently the Organic Hophead India Pale Ale.

The café has since been sold but the brewery remains in operation under the guidance of Kieran and brewer Carl Hadler, a holder of the English Brewers Guild Diploma. Carl, together with Kieran and Belinda (winemaker for Muddy Water Wines), is always looking to improve on what has been accepted in the region as good-quality beer, and to produce ales with integrity.

The 600-litre brews are pure malt, hops, yeast and well water and in the case of the Hophead India Pale Ale made from certified organic ingredients. The beer is naturally carbonated and neither filtered or pasteurised, resulting in a rich, full-flavoured product. There is some variation between batches — the mark of a brewer constantly fine-tuning his 'babies'.

Currently the beers can be purchased from the brewery and from liquor stores, cafés and wine shops around Canterbury, as well as a couple of outlets in Wellington. However, there are plans to make them more widely available.

The distinctive Brew Moon labels are the artwork of Canterbury artist Celia Allison, creator of the cartoon character 'Cecily' found in magazines and daily newspapers around New Zealand.

Located on SH 1, 40 minutes north of Christchurch, the brewery is at the gateway to Waipara, one of the fastest-growing wine regions in New Zealand, thus providing a fascinating and satisfying addition to a day of wining and dining.

AMBERLEY PALE ALE

ALCOHOL
4% abv
STYLE
New Zealand Pale Ale

Made using a combination of American yeast, European malt and American hop varieties grown in Nelson this is a freshly malty little number with a light and crisp mouth-feel. It has a distinctly herbal note that seems to derive from the particular yeast being used and a lingering bitterness towards the end. For me, while it is a well-made beer, this needs a little more body particularly in the middle palate just to round it off. However, it is easy drinking and will go well with a variety of foods, especially summer antipasto.

HOPHEAD INDIA PALE ALE

ALCOHOL
5% abv
STYLE
India Pale Ale

A much sweeter beer than the Pale Ale but with a similar herbal note, this has a pleasant bitterness with good weight and is nicely refreshing. The balance between malt and hop is admirable and the length of the palate appealing. Definitely one for those who like their beers hoppy. I recommend a glass or two with a Caesar salad.

BROOMFIELD ALE

A tawny brown colour with a tinge of red, this is an aromatic rendition with malt to the fore. The texture is moderately creamy, the mouth-feel satisfying. The taste is fairly fruity with some yeast influence and that familiar Brew Moon herbal note. As with others in the range, a hop bitterness on the back palate is evident and the aftertaste lingers. I would serve this with a mixed grill of sausages, lamb's fry and bacon for an easy and tasty dinner.

ALCOHOL
4% abv

STYLE
Red Ale

THE DARK SIDE STOUT

This strong beer looks good in the glass with its almost black colour and creamy head. It has a roasted malt aroma with a hint of Christmas cake as well. It's moderately creamy and has a roasted malt/dark chocolate flavour, the Brew Moon herbal factor, and the consistent bitter finish. I would have this with a sweet dessert to offset the bitterness; something like a caramel mousse. Alternatively, serve it up with cream cheese on dark rye bread as an appetiser.

ALCOHOL
6% abv

STYLE
Stout

DUX DE LUX

The very popular Dux de Lux bar, restaurant and lounge can be found at the Arts Centre complex in the heart of New Zealand's garden city. The Dux, as it is affectionately known, was established 15 years ago and serves up a range of packaged brews as well as its own, and also provides an extensive menu of café-style food. Owner and hospitality industry identity Richard Sinke, together with ebullient brewer Richard Fife, has a share in a Queenstown café and bar of the same name (see page 139) and a brewing philosophy of producing natural beers that are genuine and honest in ingredients and the way they are made. Their beer is

ADDRESS
41 Hereford Street, Christchurch

PHONE
(03) 366 6919

FAX
(03) 366 5341

BREWER
Richard Fife

OPEN
Daily 11.30 am– 11 pm

NEW ZEALAND
BEER LABELS

One of the things we do really well in New Zealand, apart from making beer, is branding it. For some breweries it is an intrinsic part of the marketing process; for others it is simply part of the passion and the craftmanship of creating beer. There is a huge range of designs included here – yet not all beers made in this country are represented. Some beers are served only on tap and so have no label as such. Some brewers chose to submit only a sample of their range; others were in the process of redesigning their labels.

The following pages offer a treasure trove of labels: plain and extravagant, complex and simple, multicoloured and black-and-white. Some celebrate the regional character of the beer and some the idiosyncratic nature of the brewer. In order to include as many as possible the labels have not been printed to a common scale. They are set out in the same order as the tasting notes in the book.

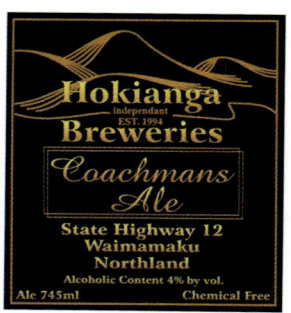

LEFT
Hokianga Breweries
p 19

RIGHT
Pilot Bay Brewing
p 21

LEFT
Pilot Bay Brewing
p 21

RIGHT
Pilot Bay Brewing
p 22

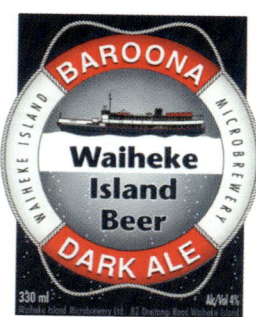

LEFT
Waiheke Island
Brewery p 23

RIGHT
Waiheke Island
Brewery p 23

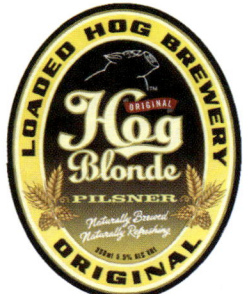

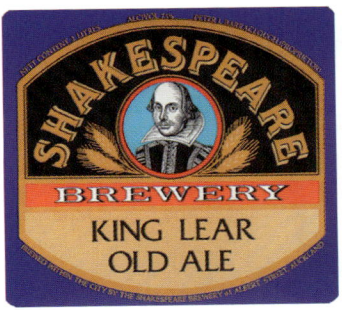

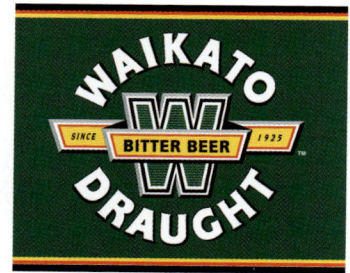

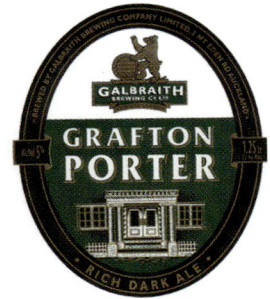

LEFT
Galbraith Brewing
Company p 35

RIGHT
Galbraith Brewing
Company p 36

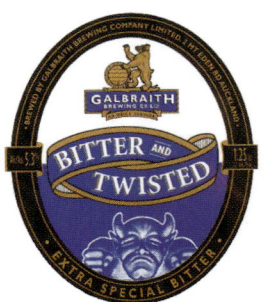

LEFT
Galbraith Brewing
Company p 36

RIGHT
Waitemata Brewery
p 39

LEFT
Waitemata Brewery
p 40

RIGHT
Waitemata Brewery
p 40

LEFT
Waitemata Brewery
p 40

RIGHT
Steam Brewing
Company p 43

LEFT
Steam Brewing
Company p 43

RIGHT
Steam Brewing
Company p 44

LEFT
Steam Brewing
Company p 44

RIGHT
Steam Brewing
Company p 45

LEFT
Steam Brewing
Company p 45

RIGHT
Independent
Brewery p 46

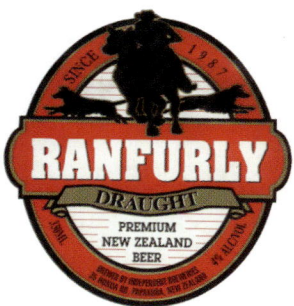

LEFT
Independent
Brewery p 46

RIGHT
Independent
Brewery p 47

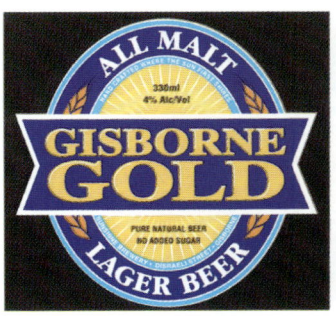

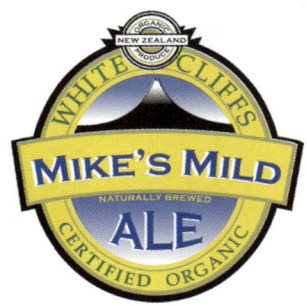

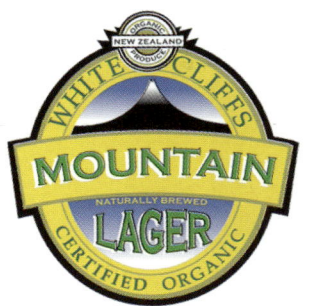

LEFT
Mates Brewery
p 51

RIGHT
Roosters Brewhouse
p 52

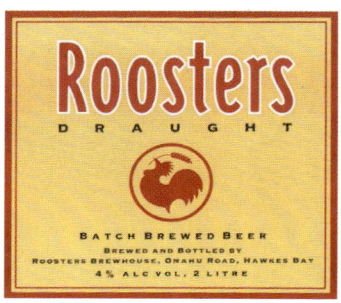

LEFT
Roosters Brewhouse
p 53

RIGHT
Roosters Brewhouse
p 53

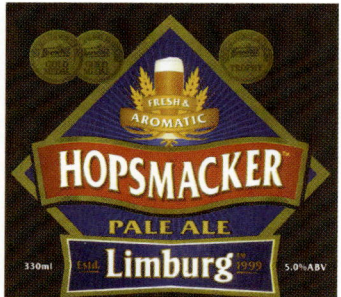

LEFT
Roosters Brewhouse
p 53

RIGHT
Limburg Brewing
Company p 54

LEFT
Limburg Brewing
Company p 55

RIGHT
Limburg Brewing
Company p 55

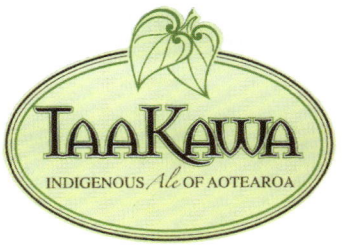

LEFT
Waituna Brewing
Company p 56

RIGHT
Tui Brewery
p 59

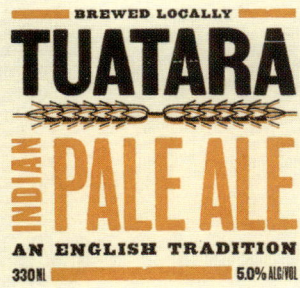

LEFT
Tuatara Brewery
p 60

RIGHT
Tuatara Brewery
p 61

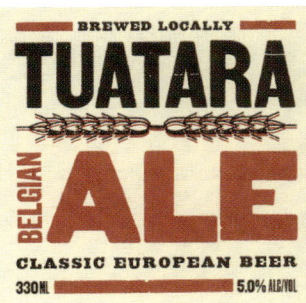

LEFT
Tuatara Brewery
p 61

RIGHT
Tuatara Brewery
p 61

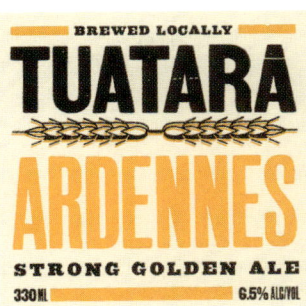

LEFT
Tuatara Brewery
p 61

RIGHT
Tuatara Brewery
p 62

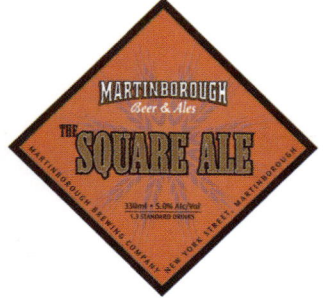

LEFT
Martinborough Beer
& Ales p 63

RIGHT
Martinborough Beer
& Ales p 63

LEFT
Martinborough Beer
& Ales p 63

RIGHT
Martinborough Beer
& Ales p 64

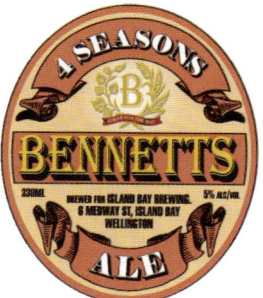

LEFT
Island Bay Brewing
Company p 65

RIGHT
Island Bay Brewing
Company p 65

LEFT
Island Bay Brewing
Company p 66

SOUTH ISLAND BREWERIES

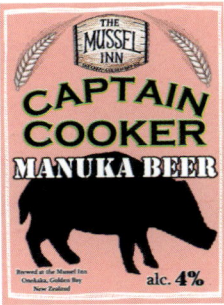

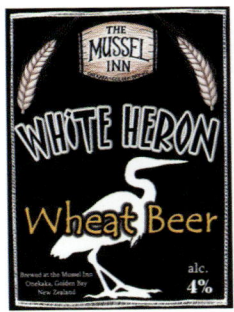

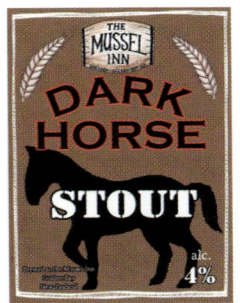

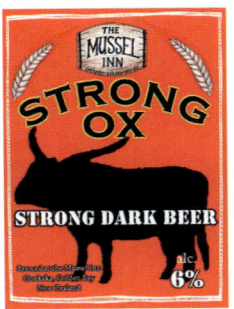

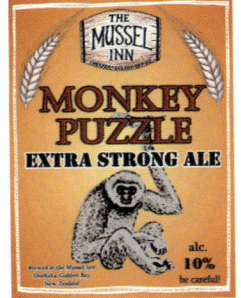

LEFT
Mussel Inn Bush
Café p 71

RIGHT
Mussel Inn Bush
Café p 71

LEFT
Mussel Inn Bush
Café p 71

RIGHT
Mussel Inn Bush
Café p 72

LEFT
Mussel Inn Bush
Café p 72

RIGHT
Mussel Inn Bush
Café p 72

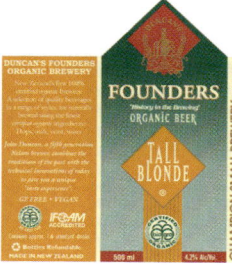
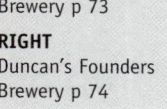

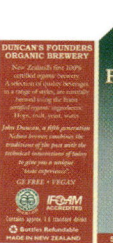

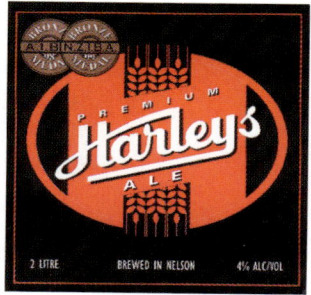

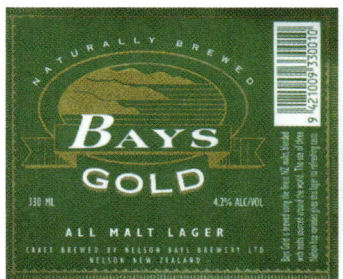

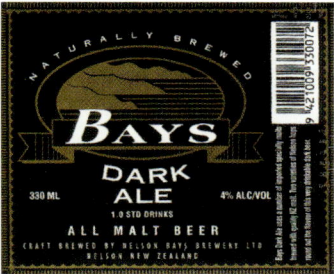

LEFT
Nelson Bays
Brewery p 77

RIGHT
Nelson Bays
Brewery p 77

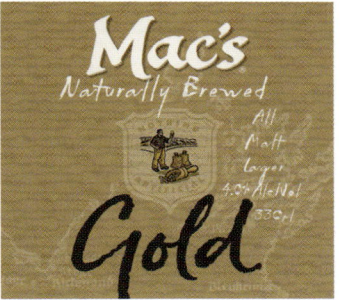

LEFT
Nelson Bays
Brewery p 78

RIGHT
Mac's Brewery
p 82

LEFT
Mac's Brewery
p 82

RIGHT
Mac's Brewery
p 83

LEFT
Mac's Brewery
p 83

RIGHT
Mac's Brewery
p 83

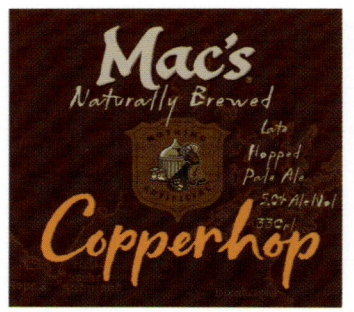

LEFT
Mac's Brewery
p 84

RIGHT
Pink Elephant
Brewery p 86

LEFT
Pink Elephant
Brewery p 86

RIGHT
Pink Elephant
Brewery p 87

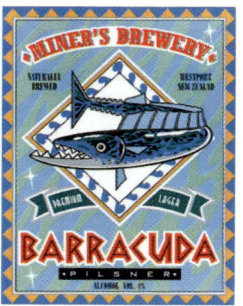

LEFT
Pink Elephant
Brewery p 87

RIGHT
Miner's Brewery
p 88

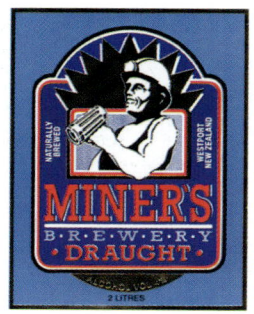

LEFT
Miner's Brewery
p 88

RIGHT
Miner's Brewery
p 88

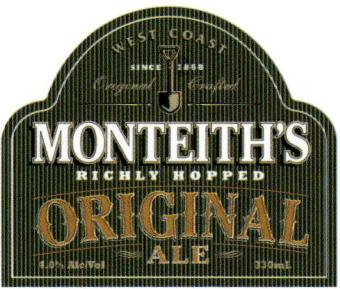

LEFT
Miner's Brewery
p 89

RIGHT
Monteith's Brewing
Company p 90

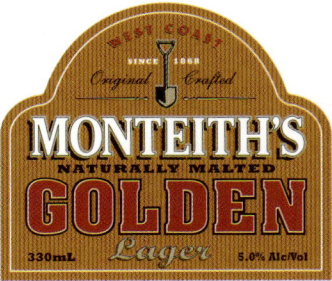

LEFT
Monteith's Brewing
Company p 91

RIGHT
Monteith's Brewing
Company p 91

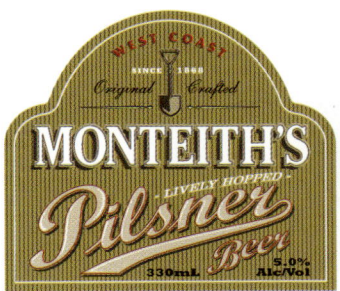

LEFT
Monteith's Brewing
Company p 91

RIGHT
Monteith's Brewing
Company p 92

LEFT
Monteith's Brewing
Company p 92

RIGHT
Monteith's Brewing
Company p 92

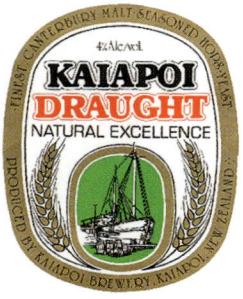

Amberley Pale Ale

Broomfield Ale

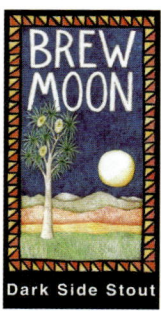

Dark Side Stout

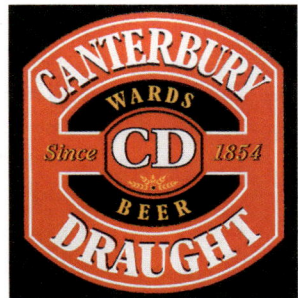

LEFT
Harrington's
Breweries p 127

RIGHT
Harrington's
Breweries p 128

LEFT
Harrington's
Breweries p 128

RIGHT
Harrington's
Breweries p 128

LEFT
Harrington's
Breweries p 129

RIGHT
Harrington's
Breweries p 129

LEFT
Harrington's
Breweries p 129

RIGHT
Matson's Brewery
Ltd p 130

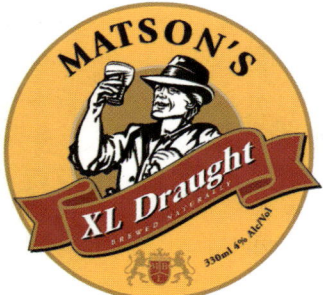

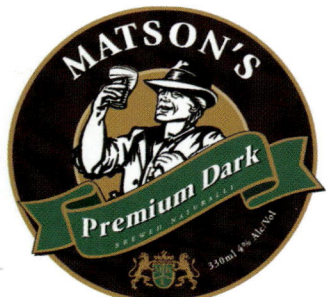

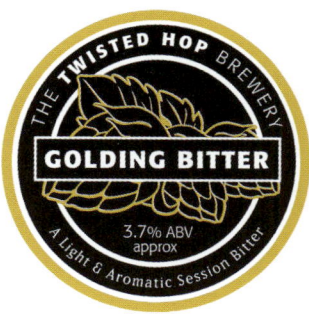

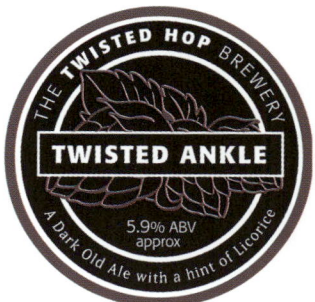

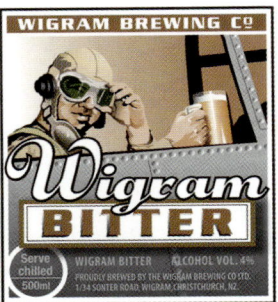

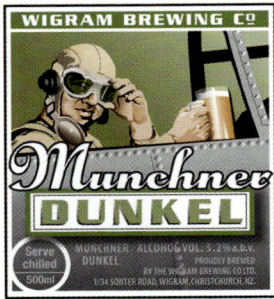

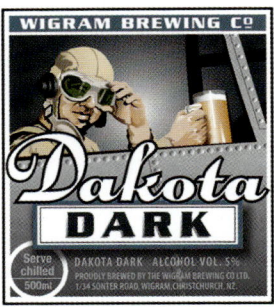

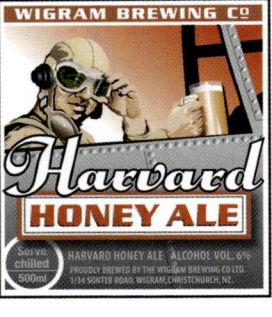

LEFT
Wanaka Beerworks
p 138

RIGHT
Wanaka Beerworks
p 139

LEFT
Wanaka Beerworks
p 139

RIGHT
BannockBrew
p 141

LEFT
BannockBrew
p 141

RIGHT
BannockBrew
p 141

LEFT
McDuffs Brewery
p 142

RIGHT
McDuffs Brewery
p 142

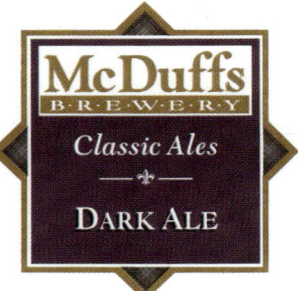

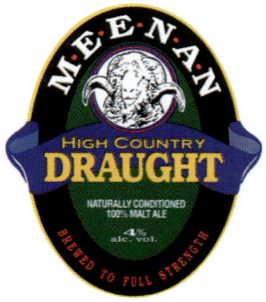

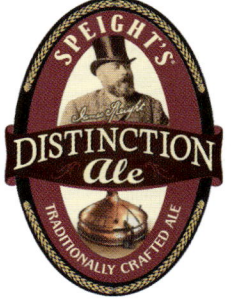

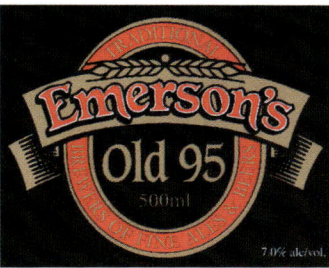

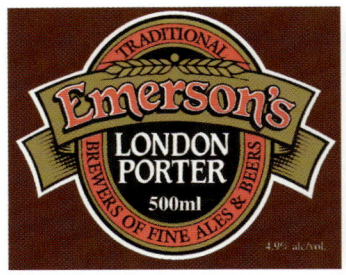

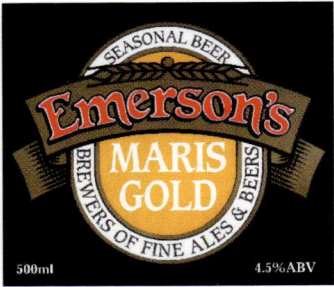

LEFT
The Emerson
Brewing Company
p 150

RIGHT
The Emerson
Brewing Company
p 150

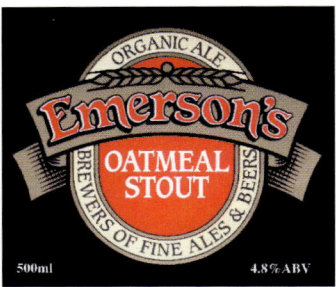

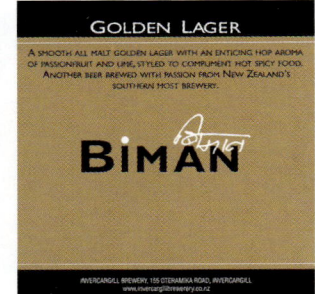

LEFT
The Emerson
Brewing Company
p 150

RIGHT
Invercargill Brewing
Company p 152

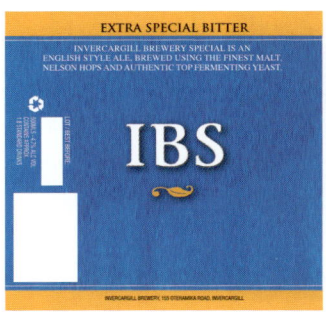

LEFT
Invercargill Brewing
Company p 152

RIGHT
Invercargill Brewing
Company p 152

brewed to appeal to those who appreciate craft-style beer and both top- and bottom-fermenting processes are used. Richard produces 4000 litres per week, catering exclusively for patrons of the Dux de Lux in spite of many requests for a bottled version. 'We have enough trouble keeping up with demand from our in-house customers,' says Richard. The range, some of which have won awards in international beer competitions, is not available anywhere else in New Zealand and can therefore be considered a unique Christchurch experience.

The guys also brew an alcoholic ginger beer — Ginger Tom — that is well worth trying; it's tasty, refreshing and satisfying, especially in the summer with fresh shellfish. There is a non-alcoholic version, which is a tad sweet for my palate but which remains extremely popular.

DUX LAGER

Pale yellow-gold with a light, distinctively white head and a low level of carbonation, this lager has an aroma of honeysuckle, mild hop and medium malt fruitiness. It is well balanced in texture, with good mouth-feel and a light hop bitterness in the pilsner style. The flavour is of crisp malt and plenty of fruit. A well-made beer with broad appeal, it is likely to be a good partner for spicy food. I would also serve it with sweet and sour pork.

ALCOHOL
4% abv

STYLE
Lager

BLUE DUCK AMBER LAGER

This beer fills the glass with a vibrant red-copper colour. There is an aroma of roasted malt with some biscuity and fruity characters as well. The texture is crisp and clean, not hearty but mouth-filling. This is an easy-drinking beer in which the malt flavours shine through and you are left with a softly chocolate aftertaste. It is a good beer to partner battered fish and chips and mushy peas.

ALCOHOL
4% abv

STYLE
Amber Lager

BEER QUOTES 'It is plain and demonstrable, that much ale is not good for Yankee, and operates differently upon them from what it does upon a Briton; ale must be drank in a fog and a drizzle.' Herman Melville (1819–91)

DUX PREMIUM LAGER

I liked this new golden straw-coloured beer, mostly for its depth of flavour and ability to satisfy my preference for balanced hop bitterness. It is a premium offering more than an intentional step above the other Dux lagers. It has a fullish body, lingering malt/hop taste and a rich aftertaste that show off the effects of late hopping very well indeed. My pick is to serve this with steamed mussels with lemon juice or in the spring with a lamb roast. Delicious!

ALCOHOL
5.5% abv

STYLE
Golden Lager

 **TOP BREW**

HEREFORD BITTER

I liked this better than at previous tastings. It has a dark ruby colour and an aroma of caramel, rhubarb crumble and mild roast coffee. The mouth-feel is light and fresh with a crisp texture and luscious mouth-feel. Coffee and malt come through as flavours and there is good length. This is a well-made traditional Kiwi-style beer with mild hop influences that kick in at the end, another to serve with grilled food — or perhaps with a rich chicken cassoulet.

ALCOHOL
4% abv

STYLE
English-style Bitter

NOR'WESTER STRONG ALE

Top-fermented in true ale style, the Nor'wester is a rich red-tan colour — almost copper — and has a sweet malt aroma with some peat and fruit. It is creamy and mouth-filling in texture and is best appreciated at room temperature. The malt comes through again as flavour and it finishes with a slightly medicinal, winey/spicy character that is very attractive. A multi-dimensional beer, well made, this would be perfect with roast beef or tasty aged cheddar.

ALCOHOL
6.5% abv

STYLE
Strong Ale

 **TOP BREW**

SOU'WESTER STRONG DARK STOUT

Made only for the winter months this beer is dark and densely coloured with a creamy head, a strong fruit malt aroma and fine texture. Although it is not mouth-filling, tending on the thinner side, there is plenty of flavour — caramel, chocolate and coffee. The toasty malt comes through on the palate and provides moderate length and will appeal to dark-beer fans more so than to creamy stout drinkers. Match it with blue cheese.

ALCOHOL
6.5% abv

STYLE
Stout

BLACK SHAG STOUT

This attractive beer is dark, almost black, with a rich, creamy head that stays and stays. The aroma is of pure malt and it intensifies as the beer warms. The texture, as you would expect, is rich and creamy with plenty of mouth-feel, the flavours big and bold with an interesting combination of chocolate, fruit and stable hay. The length is just as it should be and entices you to savour another mouthful. Choose game as a meat accompaniment; the daring might go for baklava or Russian fudge cake.

ALCOHOL
5.5% abv

STYLE
Stout

CANTERBURY BREWERY (LION BREWERIES SOUTH)

The imposing landmark that is Canterbury Brewery has been around in one state or another since 1854. It was formed as a result of mergers between three major Christchurch breweries — Wards, Crown and Mannings. By the time it became part of New Zealand Breweries in 1923, it had established an enduring business with the support of both the local community and the greater Canterbury region. Today Canterbury Brewery produces up to 50 million litres of beer per year on its 2.5-hectare site in the heart of Christchurch. A raft of brands comes out of the brewery but its flagship is Canterbury Draught, or CD, as it is known to its friends.

ADDRESS
36 St Asaph Street, Christchurch

PHONE
(03) 379 4940

FAX
(03) 371 3222

HEAD BREWER
Colin Garland

THE HERITAGE CENTRE
The Heritage Centre provides a great account of the history of brewing in the region and the country.

OPEN
Mon–Thu 10 am & 12.30 pm
Sat 1 pm

CANTERBURY DRAUGHT

Originally known as Wards Ale, Canterbury Draught is designed to satisfy today's Cantabrian, while still holding true to the traditional style of its heritage. This moderately malty beer balanced with Nelson hops and rounded out with a hint of sweetness has body and flavour

ALCOHOL
4% abv

STYLE
New Zealand Draught

while remaining easy drinking. Canterbury Draught is ideal with delicately flavoured meats such as pork, chicken and, of course, Canterbury lamb with minted potatoes.

KILKENNY

New Zealand is one of eight countries brewing this Irish beer under licence. It is distinctively ruby-red in colour, with a rich, creamy head that lasts to the end. The texture is rich and smooth with a clean and refreshing mouth-feel. It is easy drinking with plenty of malt and fruit mince character as well as a hint of caramel and molasses. I'd serve Kilkenny with game meat or with a slice of Stilton before dessert.

> **ALCOHOL**
> 4.3% abv
>
> **STYLE**
> Irish Red Ale

GUINNESS

One of the world's most popular stouts, Guinness is brewed in New Zealand under licence. A deep dark chocolate-brown in colour, it is deliciously aromatic with roasted malt and coffee notes and some toffee character as well. The texture is creamy and smooth, very soft and mouth-filling. The taste is full-on roasted malt and moderate hop, but with a tang of hop acidity and some spice and fruit too. It is a complex beer with a fresh dryness at the end — which is a long time coming, such is this beer's length. The classic match is oysters and it makes sense when in New Zealand to partner Guinness with some of our very fine Bluff, Nelson or Orongo Bay oysters.

> **ALCOHOL**
> 4.1% abv
>
> **STYLE**
> Stout

THE LOADED HOG BREWERY

The Christchurch Loaded Hog Brewery is part of a nationwide chain of restaurants/bars. The Christchurch brewery is located away from the restaurant (on the corner of Cashel and Manchester Streets in the heart of the city). The beer brewed in Christchurch is also served at the Loaded Hogs in Timaru and Queenstown. For full details and tasting notes, see pages 24–27.

> **ADDRESS**
> 39 Dundas Street, Christchurch
>
> **PHONE/FAX**
> (03) 377 2249
>
> **BREWER**
> Matthew Thompson
>
> **OPEN**
> The restaurant and bar is open daily 11 am–late

HARRINGTON'S BREWERIES

ADDRESS
99 Ferry Road,
Christchurch City

PHONE
(03) 366 6323

FAX
(03) 366 3542

EMAIL
yt@hyper.net.nz

BREWER
Mark White

OPEN
Mon–Wed 10 am–
8pm
Thu 10 am–9 pm
Fri–Sat 10 am–
10 pm

One of the larger microbreweries in New Zealand, Harrington's supplies a chain of bottle stores in Christchurch and the Canterbury region and is soon to be exported to the UK. Catering to a general audience of mainstream beer drinkers, Harrington's offers a wide selection of beers in competition with the bigger brewers.

Brewer Mark White is a genial character and one of those passionate brewers constantly working to improve his beers. I think he has succeeded and the current crop is significantly better than earlier brews. Mark knows his stuff and aims to produce high-quality beer that covers a range of flavour preferences while remaining price-competitive. Under Mark's guiding hand Harrington's beers have gained significant recognition in recent beer competitions.

There are many beers in the Harrington's range and most are widely available in both packaged and draught form from liquor retailers throughout the South Island and from the brewery itself. A number of the beers are also available from Harrington's Brewery in Nelson (see page 78), owned by Craig Harrington, son of the owner of Harrington's in Christchurch.

In addition, the company now has its own restaurant, café and bar by the same name in Belfast, a suburb of Christchurch, where you can enjoy Harrington's beers together with food from an extensive menu.

HARRINGTON'S BIG JOHN

ALCOHOL
6.5% abv

STYLE
Scottish Ale

AWARDS
Rated No. 1 by
Cuisine magazine,
2004

This award-winning ale, available in draught and packaged form, is amber-gold in colour and has a strong aroma of cut grass with a few citrus notes as well. It has a pleasantly crisp texture that fills the mouth, and is smooth but surprises with some late zestiness that creeps up on the back palate. The flavour is of malt with some hop grassiness, while the overriding impression is of an appealing fruity, almost fortified character that just when you think you have it sussed, reveals another dimension. The high alcohol content is recognisable in the dryness on the sides of the palate and some sweetness is evident on the back of the throat. This is an alluring well-balanced beer, sophisticated enough for enjoying on its own, especially well chilled, or try it at room temperature with a lamb roast complete with mint sauce. Alternatively anything slightly smoky will bring out the smokiness in the beer and play up its tempting sweetness.

HARRINGTON'S HERITAGE LAGER

ALCOHOL
4% abv
STYLE
Lager

Pale gold in colour, this beer has an aroma that is mildly hoppy with a touch of sugar sweetness to it. I tried it soon after Mark had introduced a new yeast and it was certainly making its presence felt, especially in the aroma. The texture is crisp and fresh and very fine. It's not a highly flavoured beer — it will suit those who enjoy the lighter lager style — although it has a lovely malt influence together with the necessary hop character in the finish. It's a good quaffer to enjoy when you have friends over for a pizza.

HARRINGTON'S FINEST LAGER

ALCOHOL
5% abv
STYLE
Lager

A thick, creamy head tops this hearty dark gold beer only available in draught form. It has a slightly wheaty, slightly musty aroma to it. In the mouth it is crisp and clean with an appealing freshness. The depth of flavour is good, with some malt fruit characters together with a good level of hop bitterness for this style. It's an easy-drinking, thoroughly pleasant beer that I would match with a spicy dish, perhaps a Malaysian beef curry.

HARRINGTON'S BEST BITTER

ALCOHOL
5% abv
STYLE
All Malt Lager

 TOP BREW

A favourite with the brewer, and with me, this delicious, malty brew in the English style presents beautifully in the glass with its deep tan colour and plush, creamy head that clings to the glass. Oodles of toffee and caramel character come through in both aroma and taste. The texture is clean and smooth, the depth of flavour appealing. It is well balanced and tasty and will satisfy the most discerning. I was impressed with the character of this beer and would recommend it be served with a beef casserole or a steak and kidney pie. Top marks!

HARRINGTON'S KIWI DRAUGHT

Brewed to fit into New Zealand mainstream draught style, Kiwi Draught is copper-gold and has a malty aroma with hints of caramel and old leather. It is lighter bodied with no real length, and the flavour is sweetish rather than hoppy. Sure to appeal to many New Zealand beer drinkers, this is an unpretentious big-selling quaffing beer best enjoyed with a few hot savouries while watching the rugby. It comes as a packaged product sometimes branded as South Island Draught.

ALCOHOL
4% abv
STYLE
New Zealand Draught

HARRINGTON'S DRAUGHT (TAP ONLY)

This is another copper-gold beer with similar characteristics to the earlier Draught but only available on tap. There is a little more coffee and fruit in the aroma but the smell of leather is still there. The texture is slightly creamier, but it is drier and more complex in flavour than the previous beer. The malt flavours are more pronounced and the hops more evident. For a good partner I'd suggest a mixed grill of lamb chops, bacon and beef sausages with lashings of HP Sauce.

ALCOHOL
4% abv
STYLE
New Zealand Draught

HARRINGTON'S HERITAGE DRAUGHT

Copper-brown in colour, this beer has plenty of rich malt sweetness in the aroma, as well as some honey and caramel notes. The texture is smooth rather than crisp, the flavour tending towards the mainstream but with a depth not always found in the average Kiwi brown beer. It's a perfectly reasonable session beer that you can enjoy any time of year. I would serve it with a grazing platter of salami, pickles, cheese and olives that will taste even better with the sweetness provided by this beer.

ALCOHOL
4% abv
STYLE
New Zealand Draught

HARRINGTON'S HERITAGE DARK

This beer is the colour of molasses — deep, deep copper with a hint of red — and has a thick, creamy, brown head. There is coffee and caramel in the aroma, but the hokey pokey so pronounced on the nose in earlier versions is now more evident on the palate. The texture is a little lighter than expected but there is plenty of length, with

ALCOHOL
4% abv
STYLE
Dark Lager

flavours of roast malt and dark fruit coming through. This is much smoother than earlier versions. It has more balance and better flavour, yet Mark says he is still tampering with it to get it just right. Try it with small pieces of a rich, dark fruitcake.

HARRINGTON'S BEES KNEES HONEY PALE ALE

ALCOHOL
4.7% abv
STYLE
Honey-infused Ale

There is definitely honey there but perhaps more subtle than expected given the quantity used. The honey certainly complements the malt and serves to soften any hop bitterness. I found it a bit lightweight and sweet, requiring perhaps a bit of fine-tuning to get the balance and the drinkability quotient up. Like any honey-flavoured beer it will team up effectively with pork dishes, especially those with a dash of ginger added.

HARRINGTON'S NGAHERE GOLD

ALCOHOL
7.5% abv
STYLE
Dark Lager

This is a potent brew, tan gold in colour with an unctuous creamy texture. The aroma is winey with some new pinot noir characters. It has good mouth-feel, with plenty of power at the back of the throat as you might expect. There is plenty of flavour there but it would benefit in my view with some bolstering of the middle palate where it seems to lack a little vigour. It's a popular drink but needs to be treated carefully given the higher alcohol content and most advisedly should be partnered with generous quantities of food. I would suggest hamburgers and fries.

HARRINGTON'S SILVER FERN PREMIUM LAGER

ALCOHOL
5% abv
STYLE
Lager

An attractively packaged lager that shows off the brewer's willingness to push the boundaries as much as the uniqueness of New Zealand native foliage! Made with a variety of malts and hops not used in other Harrington's products, this lager has a smooth and satisfying mouth-feel, plenty of flavour and a distinctive herb/hop character underpinning the whole. There is a good deal of residual bitterness that gives this beer real class on the finish. I would serve this with a mild curry with a level of sweetness to it or with steamed mussels.

> **BEER FACTS** The first beer purity laws date as far back as the time, 4000 years ago, when Babylonian lawgiver Hammurabi condemned brewers who made bad beer to be thrown into the river.

HARRINGTON'S MONSOON LAGER

ALCOHOL	5.6% abv
STYLE	Lager

Made specifically for enjoying with Indian food, Monsoon Lager is styled not surprisingly on the Indian Kingfisher beer although the label on the bottle in my view is far superior. It is a bright golden colour and has a delicately floral aroma with some bittersweetness to it, most likely from the hop. It is crisp with plenty of cut-through. Well balanced, with a combination of bitter and sweet that will win over even the fiercest of curries, which is exactly what I would serve it with.

HARRINGTON'S PREMIUM LAGER

ALCOHOL	5% abv
STYLE	Lager

Another version of lager, this with plenty of meaty aroma, incorporating grassy hop and malt sweetness. Good mouth weight, smooth and very drinkable as a thirst quencher. More flavour than the average sweetish New Zealand lager — evidence of good-quality ingredients being used in its production. Take with you to your favourite Mexican restaurant and enjoy in lieu of an imported lolly water that needs lime to provide flavour.

HARRINGTON'S BIG JOHN RESERVE

ALCOHOL	6.5% abv
STYLE	Amber Lager
AWARDS	Supreme Winner, New Zealand Beer Cup 2002

 **TOP BREW**

Yum! A super-premium, amber-red beer with a wonderful malt and spice aroma. Smooth and unctuous this stunner coats the whole palate with flavour. Nicely rounded, it is consistent to the end, with malt characters dominating, accentuated by a touch of bourbon flavour from 12 months' conditioning in bourbon barrels. I liked it a lot and awarded it highly amongst the Harrington's portfolio. It is one for cautious supping but the reward is a fascinating, stylish tipple with a depth of flavour that relegates so many other beers around the country into the characterless category.

MATSON'S BREWERY LTD

ADDRESS
6 Tenahaun St,
Sockburn,
Christchurch

PHONE
(03) 341 3229

BREWERS
Paul Hogan & Paul
McAllum

OPEN
Daily 11 am–late

The guys at Matson's are a friendly, easy-going lot who make no bones about the fact they brew economical, easy-drinking beers to satisfy the thirst of their customers. The range is designed as an alternative to the high volume offerings of major producers with an occasional seasonal beer made to tempt customers with something a bit unusual or special. The highly specced brewery is located behind a convivial pub in an industrial suburb of Christchurch; the beer is brewed and transported in draught form to over 80 outlets throughout the South Island. At the time of going to print a new bottling line had been commissioned with a view to producing the beer in bottles for retail sale.

MATSON'S GOLD LABEL LAGER

Standard Kiwi lager, crisp and clean, well made, sweetish with the addition of 10% wheat adding a touch of flavour interest. It's never going to have hop purists standing on the tables but it has a loyal following with Matson's customers who enjoy its easy-drinking qualities. Serve it with a spicy curry or at your next summer barbecue.

ALCOHOL
4.5% abv

STYLE
Lager

MATSON'S PREMIUM PILSENER

A combination of Czech Saaz hops and good-quality German malts help to make this a more interesting proposition than the lager. When well chilled it is crisp and refreshing, just as a good pilsner should be, but although it has some late hop it remains very approachable without the high levels of bitterness associated with European pilsners. It is a clean, easy drinking beer. I would serve it with Chinese food such as spring rolls and wontons or with Indian samosas.

ALCOHOL
5% abv

STYLE
European-style
Lager

MATSON'S XL DRAUGHT

A bright, clear beer, copper in colour and attractive in the glass. The aroma is moderately malty with some fruit mince character. Again, this is a reasonably sweet and mainstream beer intended for savouring while hanging out at the bar with mates after work. Matson's

ALCOHOL
4% abv

STYLE
New Zealand
Draught

customers wanting a bit more texture than the lagers offer claim this as their own. Almost anything from the Matson's menu will go with this unassuming quaffer but if you're feeling adventurous take some home next time you are having cottage pie or corned beef.

MATSON'S CLASSIC DRAUGHT

A typical Kiwi brown draught, red-tinged tan colour, easy drinking, reasonably creamy, malty, sweetish, inoffensive and unchallenging. It's clean and a good if unremarkable example of the style.

> **ALCOHOL**
> 4% abv
>
> **STYLE**
> New Zealand Draught

MATSON'S PREMIUM DARK

My pick from the selection, the Dark is deep chocolate in colour with a creamy, attractive head. A good balance of malt and caramel in the aroma is repeated in the taste with a touch of molasses/maple syrup. The mouth weight is good and the aftertaste lingers, leaving a coating of chocolate and caramel on the throat. The roasted, black and crystal malts raise this beer a notch and keep it interesting while at the same time preserving its ease of drinking in the Matson's style.

> **ALCOHOL**
> 4.2% abv
>
> **STYLE**
> Dark Lager

THE TWISTED HOP MICROBREWERY & BRASSERIE

Another pleasant surprise in my journey around New Zealand breweries was The Twisted Hop, which had only been open a few months when I visited. The 'baby' of two recent immigrants, Londoners Martin Bennett and Stephen Hardman, the micro-brewery is their way of dealing with the disappointment over the uninteresting and non-challenging style of beer that appeared to them to dominate the pubs and bars of Christchurch. It was by happy coincidence they met soon after arriving here with their families in 2003 and discovered they shared the same passion for bringing cask-conditioned beer to New Zealand.

While the beers are brewed in the traditional English manner

> **ADDRESS**
> 6 Poplar St, Christchurch
>
> **PHONE**
> (03) 962 3688
>
> **WEBSITE**
> www.thetwistedhop.co.nz
>
> **BREWERS**
> Martin Bennett, Stephen Hardman and Nigel Mahoney
>
> **OPEN**
> Daily 12 noon–late (summer)
> See website for winter hours

the Twisted Hop is far from being a traditional English pub. Bright, modern and architecturally liberal, the venue with its user-friendly open plan seating area and contemporary brasserie menu is already proving popular with the Christchurch café set. In fact, when I met them, the team was having trouble keeping up with demand for their beers, brewed in a specially designed brewery built in Invercargill by John Timpany, a brewer himself, who spent many weeks teaching Martin and Stephen the brewing process. Nothing has been left to chance; the barrels were imported from Europe and the hand pumps, which produce a creamy head that lasts to the bottom of the glass, from Yorkshire in England.

Using English malt and a combination of English and New Zealand hops, the beers undergo their final fermentation in the barrel that they are served from — resulting in impressively fresh beer with every element in the process easily distinguishable.

The carbonation is entirely natural, being a by-product of the ongoing fermentation. The beer is conditioned and served at 10°C; however, you can opt for slightly cooler beer.

At the time of writing the beer was only available from The Twisted Hop but the team has not ruled out packaging it for retail sale at a later date.

GOLDING BITTER

ALCOHOL
3.7% abv

STYLE
English-style
Session Beer

It's not easy to make a lager that stands out in every respect. This light tan offering with its sumptuous head does the business. There is a sweetish aroma of fresh green hops newly pulled from the vine but without overt grassiness. It has a light, crisp body that impresses with the way it accentuates the hop, especially on the middle palate. Surprisingly, it has much more flavour than many higher alcohol versions showing that alcohol does not need to replace flavour. Great bitterness levels at the end. An approachable, drinkable off-dry lager that delivers totally on its promise. Serve with a creamy fettucine dish or perhaps some steamed fresh mussels with a dash of Golding Bitter and a handful of basil thrown into the pot for good measure.

CHALLENGER

ALCOHOL
5% abv

STYLE
Medium-strength
English Bitter

A well-hopped and full-bodied special bitter, this is coppery gold in the glass, with a delightfully fresh hop aroma. It fills every nook and cranny of the mouth with the full rich tastes of its key ingredients. In amongst this was a slightly estery, vinous character that was very appealing. The flavour lasted and lasted, the bitterness lingering until the final drop. If the test of a good beer is its ability to survive strongly flavoured food then this is a winner. I had mine with a pizza smothered in pesto, anchovies, prosciutto and bocconcini. What a combo!

TWISTED ANKLE

ALCOHOL
5.9% abv

STYLE
Amber Ale

This strong dark ale is a deep amber-red colour, and like other Twisted Hop beers sports a wonderfully dense, creamy head to hold in the aroma and taste. Easy drinking, it has excellent weight, not too syrupy, which means it is enjoyable even in warmer months. In fact as much as a dark beer can be refreshing, this one certainly is. The body of the beer carries the full flavour well and there is a pleasing little dryish bite at the end. Very nice indeed and I suggest it will be an outstanding partner to duck liver pâté.

WIGRAM BREWING COMPANY

ADDRESS
Unit 1/34 Sonter
Road, Sockburn,
Christchurch

PHONE
(03) 343 4493

EMAIL
gurko@
quicksilver.net.nz

BREWERS
Joe Latimer and
Paul McGurk

OPEN
Mon–Fri 10 am–
6 pm
Sat 12 noon–5 pm

I enjoyed immensely my visit to this small brewery set in the heart of an industrial suburb of Christchurch, as much for the hospitality of Paul McGurk and his team as for the opportunity to taste the significant number of beers brewed there. There would not be a more passionate beer producer in the country and while I wonder whether the task they have set themselves to keep standards consistently high over such a large number and variety of beers is too great, there can be no doubting their enthusiasm and sheer determination.

There is no one thread running through the selection of beers from Wigram. It includes some well-made standards, some

European styles and some more experimental attempts. However, there is clear commitment to using the best quality ingredients and to operating an efficient and hygienic brewing operation. I recommend a visit to their small tasting facility but if you cannot make it, then seek out the Wigram brews at New World and Pak 'n Save supermarkets in the region and selected beer retailers throughout the South Island and in Wellington.

There is also an opportunity to try beers brewed at Wigram in some of the restaurants around Christchurch, which carry brands brewed especially for them by Wigram Brewing Company.

Note: I predict the Wigram Brewing Company labels with their aviation theme will quickly become collector's items.

WIGRAM PROPELLER LAGER

ALCOHOL
5% abv

STYLE
Pale Lager

A pale tan, slightly orange brew, with a sweetish aroma, crisp texture and refreshing finish. It is a well-made session lager with a sweet taste and moderately hoppy character, evidence of quality ingredients. A typical lager in the New Zealand style, easy drinking and good with casual food such as fish and chips, burgers or the ubiquitous pie.

WIGRAM BAVARIAN PILSNER

ALCOHOL
6% abv

STYLE
German-style
Pilsner

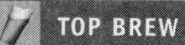 TOP BREW

A much hoppier and complex lager with appealing colour and aroma. It is crisp and tight with a nice balance of sweet and bitter. The late hopping with Technanger hops proves its value providing a lengthy bitterness on the finish. This is a good beer that will hold its own amongst more famous brands. Serve with seafood or a mild curry, which will bring out the underlying tropical fruit character in the beer.

WIGRAM BITTER

ALCOHOL
4% abv

STYLE
New Zealand
Draught

Reddy brown with little obvious aroma this is a typical New Zealand brown beer made to be easy drinking, enjoyed fresh in a number of social environments. Like others from the Wigram stable it is well made, balanced, with a malty fruit taste and a welcome kick at the end that keeps it interesting. There is more length than expected but without the hop bitterness you might expect from a true English bitter. Perfectly reasonable tipple with any red meat meal or even some aged cheddar cheese and fruit.

WIGRAM HEFE-WEIZEN

ALCOHOL	4.5% abv
STYLE	Unfiltered Wheat Beer

Wheat beers and variants on wheat beers continue to grow in popularity in New Zealand and in recognition of this Wigram is brewing its own interpretation. Pale straw in colour, cloudy, made from German pilsner malt and 70% wheat, fermented for eight days and then left for at least a week to condition, this exhibits all the hallmarks of the style. A lively tropical fruit and yeasty aroma, crisp mouth-feel to start and of moderate weight at the end, I thought it might benefit from a more substantial middle palate. Easy-drinking and tasty but in need of a little fine tuning to make it exceptional. Another to serve with shellfish or with sausages and mash.

WIGRAM MUNCHNER DUNKEL

ALCOHOL	5.2% abv
STYLE	Dark Lager

A very approachable dark beer that immediately impresses with its thick, creamy head and rich red-brown colour. It needs to be slightly warmer than when I tried it to allow the full effect of the malty aroma to manifest. The palate is well balanced, the mouth-feel creamy. Delicate Marmite/coffee and caramel tastes predominate with a fruity sweetness underpinning the whole. It's well made with plenty of appealing aftertaste that seems to linger and linger. Very nice indeed. Consider serving it with braised sausages.

WIGRAM DAKOTA DARK

ALCOHOL	5% abv
STYLE	New World Black Beer

Another good-looking beer, richly deep brown with a flamboyantly creamy head. An aroma of bittersweet chocolate with a touch of cold coffee. Nicely weighted, the texture is very smooth and it fills the mouth with a soft mousse. As suggested by the aroma, there's oodles of roasted malt fruitiness and bittersweet chocolate tastes that last and last. This would make an ideal winter warmer but will work any time of year with good-quality steak and caramelised onions.

WIGRAM HARVARD HONEY ALE

ALCOHOL
6% abv
STYLE
Honey-infused Lager

You can smell the honey aroma of this beer well in advance of putting your nose to the glass. It's rich tan in colour and sports a luxurious, creamy head. The texture is light, the mouth-feel is generous with the rata and manuka honey taste easily identifiable. There is also evidence of caramel and malt flavours, which nicely offset the honey sweetness. It's a fascinating offering that will not be everyone's first choice but one well worth trying. Finding an ideal food match will be something of an adventure but I would begin with fresh fruit salad or a chocolate mousse.

SPRUCE BEER

ALCOHOL
5% abv
STYLE
Flavoured Lager

In many ways the most interesting of all the Wigram brews but perhaps not the most palatable. Made initially for a local restaurant, the Spruce beer is based as closely as possible on a recipe from the journals of Captain James Cook, reputedly the first to brew beer in this country. Cook used the beer as a means of warding off scurvy amongst his crew. It has a herbal, almost medicinal flavour with strong molasses overtones. One glass was enough for me but it was nowhere near as 'rough' as I expected. In keeping with its origins I would serve it with a strongly flavoured dish — perhaps wild pork smoked over a bush campfire.

WIGRAM HARD HILLS MEAD

ALCOHOL
11% abv
STYLE
Mead

The team at Wigram Brewing Company sums up their beer philosophy as making product 'by beer fanatics for fanatical beer lovers'. In none of their brews is this more evident than in the high-octane mead on offer from the brewery. Heady, tasty and very effective this is one to be cautious of even though the alcohol content is lower than that of most wines. I liked it for its plentiful character and interest, its honey-ish taste and its provocative finish. My advice for a food match is that it doesn't really matter what you eat; just make sure there is plenty of it!

BEER QUOTES 'God has a brown voice, as soft and full as beer.' Anne Sexton (1928–74)

DB MAINLAND BREWERY

ADDRESS
Sheffield Street,
Washdyke, Timaru

PHONE
(03) 688 2059

FAX
(03) 688 2225

BREWERS
Beth Armstrong &
Peter Cope

Mainland Brewery is a joint venture between DB Breweries and eight South Island licensing trusts. It was built to meet the demand for DB beers in the south and the green-fields site at Washdyke, near Timaru, was ideally located for servicing the trusts' hotels and taverns. At the time there was much debate over whether to build a conventional batch-fermentation brewery or use the revolutionary continuous-fermentation process developed by Morton Coutts in the 1950s. Directors opted for continuous fermentation, which allows a constant flow of ingredients through the brewery, producing beer 24 hours a day to a consistent quality at a lower cost than batch brewing. All beer produced by DB here and at the company's other sites are microfiltered.

While other DB Breweries products are brewed at Mainland, it is DB Draught for which it is best known. This beer is available throughout the country.

DB DRAUGHT

ALCOHOL
4% abv

STYLE
All Malt Lager

A crystal-clear copper-gold in colour, this beer has a floral and malt aroma with both sweet fruit and mild hop influences. The texture is moderately creamy with a clean, refreshing appeal. Full malt flavours dominate at first — these become more raisiny on the middle palate. It has a generous mouth-feel that takes the residual sweetness on to the finish. An honest rendition of the Kiwi brown-beer style, popular with traditionalists, this beer will feel at home with no-nonsense fare such as meat pies, hearty steaks, roasts and casseroles.

VITA-STOUT

ALCOHOL
4% abv

STYLE
Stout

A deep, dark brown in colour, Vita-Stout was originally a milk stout. Over time it has developed more dryness, although it remains on the sweetish side of the ledger. A combination of roasted and chocolate malts provide the required depth of flavour and bitterness and a dryness that makes this a much easier drink than you might expect.

It comes in small bottles with very traditional — some may argue, old fashioned — labelling. But, if you are looking for an off-dry stout, Vita-Stout is unlikely to disappoint.

WANAKA BEERWORKS

Wanaka Beerworks is situated next to the Wanaka Transport Museum, about seven minutes' drive from Wanaka township. It is the dream-child of American Dave Gillies.

When I first met Dave in 1998 his operation was very new but through determination and sheer hard work, plus some important national recognition of his beers via awards, he has built Wanaka Beerworks into a highly respected brand.

Dave enthusiastically follows a European philosophy of brewing. Adhering to the Reinheitsgebot, the Bavarian beer purity law of 1516, which countenances no use of chemicals, preservatives, artificial colourings or other adjuncts, this brewery offers a natural, hand-crafted product. He brews a high-quality lager and two more specialised beers, and regularly surprises customers with a limited release, seasonal style. The impressively packaged products are available in liquor stores throughout Central Otago and further afield from selected beer retailers, and in local pubs, including the Kingsway and the Luggate Arms in Wanaka, and the Briar & Thyme in Alexandra.

ADDRESS
SH6, Wanaka

PHONE
(03) 443 1865

FAX
(03) 443 1862

Freephone 0800 Brewski OR 0800 273 975

EMAIL
wanakabeerworks@xtra.co.nz

WEBSITE
www.wanakabeerworks.co.nz

BREWER
Dave Gillies

OPEN
Daily 9 am–5 pm

BREWSKI

Wheat-gold in colour, when poured this beer offers an impressive thick, creamy, white head. The aroma is grassy with citrus fruit and honey flavours in evidence as well. There is plenty of body in this creamy beer that tastes of honey and malt with a well-balanced hop bitterness on the back palate. It will be enjoyed as an aperitif — or try it with pizza or an antipasto platter so you can experience the different levels of flavour.

ALCOHOL
4.8% abv

STYLE
Belgian-style Lager

TALL BLACK

ALCOHOL
4.8% abv
STYLE
German-style Black Lager

This is a dark brown-black beer with a thick, creamy head. Best served at room temperature for total enjoyment, it has an aroma that is strongly caramel with a slight mealiness as well. The texture is lighter than the colour might suggest and it is fresh and clean in the mouth. The flavours are complex, with chocolate, caramel and toffee all in evidence. The slightly higher alcohol content adds weight and a little dryness to the beer and gives it yet another dimension. Enjoy it as is or with fruit desserts.

CARDRONA GOLD

ALCOHOL
4.8% abv
STYLE
Vienna-style Lager

It's great to come across a beer with a totally honest label. This beer is described on the label as 'a golden lager of quaffable contingencies' and that's exactly what it is — a highly drinkable, tasty beer with mass appeal, probably best consumed as a cool and refreshing thirst quencher over the summer. But don't be fooled by the modesty of the labelling: like the others in the Wanaka Beerworks range this is a well-brewed, well-balanced beer. Enjoy it with salad, barbecue meats or a cold chicken sandwich.

DUX DE LUX

ADDRESS
14 Church Street, Queenstown
PHONE
(03) 442 9688
BREWER
Richard Fife
OPEN
Daily 11 am–late

In 1993 Steve Hagerty and Paul Graf established McNeills Cottage Brewery as a brew-pub in a historic stone building close to the centre of Queenstown. It became a popular meeting place for locals and tourists alike, people who relished trying beers different from the mainstream in a small brewery environment.

Since the last edition of the guide there has been a change of ownership and the venue has been renamed Dux de Lux, signifying the involvement of the proprietors of the bar and brewery of the same name in Christchurch. However, the original ambience has remained and the venue remains as much of an attraction as it ever was with beer still brewed on site.

The beers offered represent a combination of those brewed in Christchurch and some unique to Queenstown. A taut and tasty Alpine Ale is the local version of the Blue Duck Amber Lager (see page 121) and Queenstown also has its own locally brewed version of the Nor'wester Strong Ale and the Black Shag Stout, all brewed under the watchful eye of Dux de Lux brewer Dick Fife, who says the Queenstown water is ideal for the ale styles.

A selection of seasonal beers such as the fruit-driven Blueberry Brown Ale complements the range.

BANNOCKBREW

I have yet to visit this new brewery in the lower half of the South Island. The brewery shares its site and some of its management resources with a well-known wine producer, Akarua Wines, in Bannockburn, Central Otago. Neighbours Warren Jackson and Crawford Brown, both with strong pedigrees in the New Zealand brewing industry, came together with Dave Scott, previously Akarua vineyard manager, to give the region its own brew.

Central Otago has a proud heritage for brewing, dating back to the gold-mining era. This connection hasn't been lost on the local community, which has happily welcomed the advent of a local brewery. The trio believed it was impossible to ignore their own experience and passion for brewing beer and felt that integrating a craft brewery with the winery and restaurant added another interesting dimension to their business.

While the project was initiated a couple of years ago, Wild Spaniard beer has only been available since April 2004 and to date distribution has been limited to the Central Otago region, although there are plans to extend distribution once things have settled and the brand is better established.

ADDRESS
Rapid Number 210, Cairnmuir Road, Bannockburn, Central Otago

PHONE
(03) 445 0897

MOBILE
027 472 7889

FAX
(03) 445 0898

EMAIL
beer@akarua.com

BREWER
Dave Scott

Note: In botanical terms Wild Spaniard is a handsome-looking native herb that grows in the tussock-clad high country of Central Otago and other arid regions of New Zealand. Rosettes of extremely tough leaves and razor-sharp points are capable of cutting leather boots to shreds and severely lacerating horses' hooves. Over millions of years, the Wild Spaniard has perfectly adapted to Central Otago conditions — it can shrug off the heat of summer and happily resides in winter snowdrifts. Wild Spaniard is also the name chosen for a new range of beers crafted by BannockBrew.

WILD SPANIARD PILS

ALCOHOL
5% abv

STYLE
Czech-style Pilsner

This premium lager has been designed to showcase New Zealand's best hops against a background of soft, clean malt. The discerning beer drinker will recognise the influence of Czech pilsner, and that is entirely intentional. Both bittering and aromatic hops are used, and the technique of 'late hopping' using Hallertau and Green Bullet hops gives the beer its floral and spicy aroma.

WILD SPANIARD BEST BITTER

ALCOHOL
5% abv

STYLE
English Bitter

Here the brewer has emulated the flavour and character to be found in the very best bitters of England. A hint of roasted malt gives to the beer a warm, coppery glow, with a deep rich taste that lingers on the palate. The use of premium Nelson hops ensure a balanced bitterness able to quench all raging thirsts. And it is stronger than most of today's English bitters!

WILD SPANIARD BLACK LAGER

ALCOHOL
5% abv

STYLE
Dark Lager

With this Austrian-style beer, the accent is on warm, chocolatey, roasted flavours best described as simply luscious! Several different malts, kilned at differing temperatures, ensure a complex taste with a hint of natural sweetness. The hops are restrained to complement the malt flavours, not overpower them.

BEER QUOTES 'Beer that has not been drunk has missed its vocation.' Meyer Breslau, 1880

MCDUFFS BREWERY

ADDRESS
695 Great King Street, Dunedin

PHONE/FAX
(03) 477 7276

BREWER
Gavin Duff

OPEN
Mon–Sat 11 am–8 pm

After many years as a mechanic, Gavin Duff opened a brewery and now produces beers designed to appeal to the Kiwi brown-beer drinker. The brewery, previously known as Duffs, has been operating in Dunedin's Great King Street since August 1997. The range is available throughout Central Otago and Southland, in some cafés in Dunedin, and from the brewery itself. Gavin has a very loyal following and sees no reason to make any great changes to what is working well. However, he is constantly striving to improve his beers and reward his customers with high quality brews. In addition, he has added a couple of extra styles to the permanent range in response to very positive feedback to some seasonal brews. The first is a dark beer called Black Diamond (5%) and the second is a true-to-style stout, McDuffs Premium Stout (6.5%). I did not have the opportunity to try these but Gavin assures me they are already very popular, especially the Stout, which he says is attracting customers from far and wide.

Note: A McDuffs website is being designed and should be up and running by the time this guide is published.

MCDUFFS CLASSIC GOLD

ALCOHOL
4% abv

STYLE
Lager

Pale straw in colour, this is lightweight in the lager style. The aroma is definite wheat/barley — freshly baled hay also comes to mind. It has a good, solid mouth-feel and a medium degree of carbonation that comes from conditioning and a top-up of carbonation after fermentation. The finish is crisp and clean, and once again the strong wheat influences are to the fore. It is best drunk as an aperitif.

MCDUFFS ORIGINAL ALE

ALCOHOL
4% abv

STYLE
Lager

This light brown beer has a very slight hop aroma. The mouth-feel is good, with a distinctly grassy flavour and a hint of spiciness. It is a lightweight beer with low flavour levels, appealing to those looking for a good quaffer — try it with grilled marinated steak.

MCDUFFS EDINBURGH DRAUGHT

An interesting burnt-orange tinge makes this an attractive beer in the glass, especially when well poured with a substantial, creamy head. It has a strong aroma of hops and the hop bitterness comes through in the taste as well. It has a dry finish with a lingering bitterness that will be attractive to some. Easy drinking as a session beer, it would also be good with meat off the grill.

ALCOHOL
4% abv
STYLE
New Zealand Draught

MCDUFFS DARK ALE

This is a dark beer, almost black in colour, with a distinctive, wheaty smell about it. Lighter in texture than you might expect, it is best drunk at room temperature. The flavour brings to mind iced coffee, with only a slight fruitiness. In fact, coffee lovers are sure to enjoy this offering, and for something different I would serve it with homemade ginger slice.

ALCOHOL
4% abv
STYLE
Dark Lager

MEENAN WINES & SPIRITS LTD

Established as a family business venture in June 1997, this brewery is part of a Dunedin retail liquor outlet carrying the same name. Head brewer Stuart Littlejohn aims to produce beers that will appeal to a wide audience of local beer drinkers. Over the years he has succeeded in building a reputation for brewing beer that is consistent in flavour and texture and continues to foster and satisfy a strong local following in pubs and clubs throughout Central Otago and Southland. Meenan beer is an easy to drink, reasonably priced alternative to most if not all mainstream New Zealand beers. The range is available from Meenan Wines & Spirits.

ADDRESS
750 Great King Street, Dunedin North
PHONE
(03) 477 2047
FAX
(03) 477 2049
BREWER
Stuart Littlejohn
OPEN
Mon–Fri 8.30 am–6 pm
Sat 8.30 am–7 pm

MEENAN LAGER

ALCOHOL
5% abv
STYLE
Lager

Pale gold to straw in colour, this highly carbonated, lightweight beer in the lager style has a honey and hop aroma that is also slightly yeasty. It is smooth and crisp with a characteristic hint of citrus from the Hallertau hops used in its production. A sweet finish means it will be a good quaffing beer to refresh the palate after spicy food.

MEENAN FINEST BEST BITTER

ALCOHOL
4% abv
STYLE
English-style Bitter

Dark copper with a good, creamy head, Meenan Finest Best Bitter shines when drunk at just under room temperature. There is an easily discernible smoky peat aroma that comes through in the flavour. With little hop flavour evident, the malt provides a hint of sweet coffee, especially on the middle palate, while adding an interesting dryness. The flavour fades quickly, making it an easy-drinking beer, ideal for accommodating a variety of beer preferences. It would be perfect for barbecues.

MEENAN HIGH COUNTRY DRAUGHT

ALCOHOL
4% abv
STYLE
New Zealand Draught

Another mainstream offering, this beer is dark chocolate in colour and has a reasonably strong hop aroma. It has well-rounded texture — smooth and with plenty of body, in the style of an English ale. Toasted malts have been added, so there is a bittersweet element to this beer that means it makes good drinking with red meat. Try it with biltong or smoked beef jerky.

MEENAN EXTRA STRONG ALE

ALCOHOL
5% abv
STYLE
Strong Lager

My favourite from the Meenan selection, this dark, almost black beer is rich but not perhaps as creamy as expected. Rather it is crisp and clean and can be enjoyed well chilled. The aroma is yeasty with toasted malt characters, and this comes through as a roasted, almost burnt-toast flavour and a rather dry finish. I would be tempted to serve this interesting offering with a strong cheese — stilton perhaps.

BEER QUOTES 'I'm off for a quiet pint — followed by 15 noisy ones.' Gareth Chilcott (1956–)

SPEIGHT'S BREWERY (LION BREWERIES NEW ZEALAND)

ADDRESS
200 Rattray Street,
Dunedin

PHONE
(03) 477 9480

FAX
(03) 477 9489

WEBSITE
www.speights.co.nz

TOURS
Mon–Sun 10 am,
11.45 am & 2 pm
Mon–Thu 7 pm

Established in 1876 and located in the heart of Dunedin, Speight's Brewery is part of the Lion Breweries New Zealand group of companies and survives with much fascinating history and a very stable workforce. The locals are fiercely loyal to Speight's products and the brewery returns the compliment by being an active partner in many local and provincial community activities. Over recent years Speight's beers have gained some popularity outside the brewery's home region — they are also brewed in Lion Breweries' Auckland and Christchurch plants — but nowhere are they better received than in Dunedin, South Canterbury and Southland. These beers all have their own character. They are mainstream, with broad appeal, but also have something a little extra, which is no doubt what endears them to lovers of the classic New Zealand beer styles.

Since the last edition of this guide, Speight's has expanded its range with the Speight's Craft Range, which includes a pale ale, pilsner and porter, in addition to Speight's Distinction. These have significantly increased awareness of the brand outside its home region and garnered a wider audience enthusiastic about the full flavour of the additional styles.

Speight's Brewery's products are widely available throughout the country in both packaged and draught form. If you visit the Dunedin brewery, make sure you allow time to take a tour through the Speight's Heritage Centre, a wonderful brewing museum.

SPEIGHT'S GOLD MEDAL ALE

ALCOHOL
4% abv

STYLE
Golden Lager

The 'Pride of the South' has been brewed in Dunedin since 1876, supplying the palate preferences of what has come to be known as the 'southern man'. Copper-gold in colour, this beer has plenty of malt sweetness in the aroma as well as some grassiness. It has a fresh bouquet. The texture, too, is light and clean, and the flavour, in keeping with the aroma, is malty with medium sweetness, slightly mealy and with reasonably grassy notes as well. There is plenty of finish — overall, it is a well-balanced quaffer with broad appeal. A good choice with meat dishes, it would also appeal with more gamey variants, such as venison, duck and rabbit.

SPEIGHT'S OLD DARK

ALCOHOL
4% abv

STYLE
Malt Ale

The colour of this beer is a lovely dark brown with a red hue, the aroma full of malt with dark chocolate, butterscotch and caramel influences. The texture is luscious and full, with lots of body. Rich malt and fruit prevail in the flavour, which is not as sweet as you might expect and is balanced by hop bitterness. It is fresh and clean with good length and a touch of dryness on the back palate to keep it interesting. Like all the Speight's range it will go well with red meat, but I would recommend drinking it with a hot, rich dessert such as steamed pudding with clotted cream.

SPEIGHT'S PILSENER

ALCOHOL
5% abv

STYLE
Czech-style Lager

This tasty brew is based on a 1955 Speight's Brewery recipe and is quite possibly the star in the Speight's classic range. It's definitely one for those who appreciate hops. There is plenty of underlying malt fruit from the Munich malt to balance the significant hop content provided by the blend of Nelson Sauvin and New Zealand Saaz hops added late in the brew and which contribute plenty, particularly to the aroma. It's a clean, satisfying beer with more flavour than many in the same style brewed in New Zealand. Team it with steamed mussels or perhaps with a zesty Madras curry when its fruit will be appreciated most.

SPEIGHT'S PALE ALE

ALCOHOL
4.5% abv

STYLE
New World Pale Ale

 TOP BREW

Another brew that has its origins in an old Speight's Brewery recipe, this rendition is fermented in kauri gyles — open-topped, wooden fermentation vats which are lined with beeswax. The ale is pale gold in colour and has an appealing malt and hop aroma with a distinctive cereal/biscuit character. The taste is light caramel with a moderate bitterness provided by late hopping with Super Alpha and Saaz hops grown in the Nelson region. It has a moderate palate weight with a strength of flavour not picked up at previous tastings. However, it remains more subtle than some traditional English India Pale Ales and tends to the fruitier end of the scale. It's clean and crisp and very drinkable. To taste it at its best, serve it with meat pie and vegetables.

SPEIGHT'S DISTINCTION ALE

ALCOHOL
5% abv
STYLE
All Malt Lager

Speight's 115th anniversary was commemorated with the aptly named Distinction Ale. Intended as a single-batch brew, it proved so popular its production was continued. It has a dark copper hue with a tinge of red, and a thick, creamy head. It's quite fruity on the nose with some esters evident. The texture is crisp and clean and there is plenty of mouth-feel. The full flavour is a good balance of malt and hop, with hints of caramel and butterscotch. There is good length and a mild, pleasantly dry aftertaste. It holds its own with any full-flavoured main course. Try it with a favourite casserole.

SPEIGHT'S PORTER

ALCOHOL
5% abv
STYLE
Porter

Like a couple of its sister brews the Porter is fermented in kauri gyles and is based on a double-malt stout recipe brewed until 1929 at Speight's Brewery. It is a substantial beer with good mouth-feel and plenty of character. Its dark brown colour makes it attractive in the glass while a blend of crystal, caramalt, roasted wheat and chocolate malt combine to give a complex, smoky aroma. On the palate, flavours of dark cooking chocolate make their presence felt, while the finish has more coffee influences. It's reasonably robust and will stand up to rich meat dishes, such as barbecued spare ribs, or something more gamey, such as venison. You might also like to serve it with oysters or a well-aged cheddar.

THE EMERSON BREWING COMPANY LTD

ADDRESS
9 Grange Street,
Dunedin

PHONE
(03) 477 1812

EMAIL
brewer@
emersonsbrewery.
co.nz

WEBSITE
www.emersonsbrewery.
co.nz

BREWER
Richard Emerson

OPEN
Mon–Fri 9 am–5 pm

Travelling through the UK and Europe, Richard Emerson came to love the huge variety of fuller-flavoured beers he found there. On returning to Dunedin he set about producing similar beers, true to style, that would appeal to the palates of fine-beer drinkers in New Zealand. Along the way he aims to further educate the Kiwi beer drinker to appreciate the diversity in beer styles. The Emerson Brewing Company has been operating since 1992 and has earned a huge band of followers all over the country. The beers have received awards both here and inter-nationally, ensuring that the Emerson's brand goes from strength to strength. Such is the respect with which Richard is held in the industry that he sits on the judging panel of the BrewNZ New Zealand Beer Awards.

Richard's efforts have also attracted favourable comments on more than one occasion from Michael Jackson, the world's foremost beer writer.

Richard is something of a perfectionist. He refuses to pasteur-ise his beer and he leaves the yeast alive in the beer, to mature and complement the flavour. In an effort to ensure consumers get his beer in the best possible condition Richard transports his beers to outlets in imported French oak barrels.

Emerson's beers can be purchased direct from the brewery in PETs, kegs and in packaged form, and are now widely avail-able in good liquor stores nationwide. A selection can also be found in the beautifully refurbished Criterion Hotel in Oamaru. Emerson's beers are also available by mail order.

Each March Richard releases Taieri George (6.8% abv), while in September he releases the Emerson's American Pale Ale (6% abv). If visiting the brewery be sure to ask Richard or his staff if he has any special brews he is willing to let you try! You never know what he has on the brew out the back.

BEER QUOTES 'I've only been in love with a beer bottle and a mirror.' Sid Vicious (1957–79)

EMERSON'S 1812 INDIA PALE ALE

ALCOHOL
4.9% abv

STYLE
India Pale Ale

 **TOP BREW**

A wonderful example of the style, this India Pale Ale is brown-gold in colour with a rich aroma of spring grass and a hint of malt sweetness. It is easy drinking with a mouth-filling texture and a true English ale hop bitterness that gives the middle/back palate a real wake-up call. It's robust enough to accompany red-meat dishes, especially those with earthy flavours.

EMERSON'S PILSENER

ALCOHOL
4.9% abv

STYLE
Pilsner

One of very few truly organic beers, this pilsner is lime-gold with a delicate aroma of herbs and spices. With slight carbonation resulting from filtration, this pilsner has a gentle maltiness with a mild bitterness. A fresh, crisp offering with a good hoppy finish, it is a complex but well-balanced beer with lovely lager characteristics. It will partner any spicy Asian food, as well as full-flavoured pasta dishes.

EMERSON'S WEISSBIER HEFE-WEIZENBIER

ALCOHOL
5% abv

STYLE
Wheat Beer

Drinkers not familiar with wheat beers should not allow themselves to be put off by the cloudy character of this award-winning offering. Pale gold with a distinct aroma of Juicyfruit chewing gum, it is crisp and clean with a lingering tropical-fruit flavour balanced by a slight hop astringency. It needs to be drunk at room temperature to be fully appreciated, and makes great drinking as an aperitif or with blue cheese.

EMERSON'S BOOKBINDER BITTER

ALCOHOL
3.7% abv

STYLE
Bitter

 **TOP BREW**

Dark copper in colour, this true bitter has a gentle aroma reminiscent of blackcurrant with a touch of yeastiness. It pours with a lovely, lingering head. The texture is creamy and rich with a mild refined graininess. It has a comparatively low alcohol content and a full, malty flavour, and surprises at the end with a dash of citrus just to keep the palate fresh. It is a complex beer best served before a meal or as a partner to hearty meat dishes. This beer is available from the brewery but has limited distribution in other places.

EMERSON'S OLD 95

ALCOHOL
7% abv

STYLE
Old English Ale

 **TOP BREW**

The colour of golden syrup, with a red tint, this seasonal beer has an aroma that conjures up memories of Mum's steamed pudding. It has a rich, creamy texture with a big, buxom mouth-feel. A slightly burnt flavour (not the same toastiness as toasted malt), a hint of orange and definite fruitcake characters dominate. Great on its own, it would also pair well with any game meat and gutsy gravy.

EMERSON'S LONDON PORTER

ALCOHOL
4.9% abv

STYLE
Porter

Almost black in the bottle, this true-to-style porter pours as a very dark brown beer with plenty of fruity aroma and a creamy texture. It is a 'big' beer with lots of character. Its gentle hop bitterness is balanced by an equal weight of maltiness. The alcohol comes through as well, giving the beer some extra kick right at the end. It is another complex and full-flavoured offering to be enjoyed equally with lamb roasts or meat pies.

EMERSON'S MARIS GOLD

ALCOHOL
4.5% abv

STYLE
Lager

A seasonal lager brewed with Richard Emerson's usual flair, this brew has a golden colour and a sweet tropical malt aroma with a decent hit of hop attached. It is crisp and clean, with complex layers of bittersweet flavour that excite the palate to the last. The hop character is dominant but in no way out of balance or overpowering. It's a classy beer that will have much wider appeal than some of Richard's more esoteric brews. For a food match, I would put it with osso bucco or perhaps a succulent cut of white veal.

EMERSON'S OATMEAL STOUT

ALCOHOL
4.8% abv

STYLE
Oatmeal Stout

 **TOP BREW**

The colour of this delicious beer is best described as chocolate-brown, and it has a fruit and chocolate aroma. The classically smooth mouth-feel engulfs the palate with roasted malt caramel and chocolate tastes. There is plenty of alcohol warmth in this brew but very low-level bitterness, which is just as it should be. The mealiness you might expect in an oatmeal stout is very gentle and contributes aroma and some texture but no graininess. Try it with lamb and mint sauce.

INVERCARGILL BREWING COMPANY

ADDRESS
155 Oteramika
Road, Invercargill

PHONE
025 932 056

BREWER
Steve Nally

OPEN
Sat 11 am–3 pm, or
by arrangement

Brewer Steve Nally tells his story best:

'About 1983 I was reading the *New Zealand Listener*, and I came across a home-brewing advertisement in the classifieds. I asked Dad if we could give making beer a crack, which we did and it tasted like crap. This didn't deter me. Later, while in a supermarket, I discovered a box of hops with recipes for beer on the back. I bought a large tin of Maltexo, went home, brewed up some beer and this time it tasted great!

'During my travels overseas I discovered that beer is not always brown, fizzy, tasteless stuff but an incredibly diverse, flavoursome beverage. I also "found" cider, or I should say cider found me.

'I arrived back in New Zealand with the intention of making cider. Dad was keen and I enticed some friends to help making our first 200-litre batch. We drove around Southland going to farmers who had old apple trees growing but did nothing with the apples. We took them back to Dad's house, made one hell of a mess extracting the juice and fermented it to cider. This happened for a few years but at the same time I was home-brewing full mash beers with some success.

'We started looking for and building some equipment to start a bona fide brewery — which at this time was located in my parents' garage. Space restrictions meant this wasn't ideal so we started looking for somewhere to carry on this "hobby". The Oteramika site became available and made it possible for us to grow to where we are now.'

The brewery makes 1200 litres of beer per month in addition to its 2800-litre batch of cider per year. The beer is available from the brewery and from around 70 outlets throughout the South Island, although availability is increasing each week.

One important thing to note is the outstanding quality of the Invercargill Brewing Company labels, which in my opinion rate as truly unique among New Zealand beer labels.

BIMAN

ALCOHOL
5.2% abv

STYLE
Golden Lager

A pale straw, easy-drinking lager that offers up a fruity aroma, a soft texture and an interesting combination of flavours. It is well balanced with a definite fruity taste and a gently hoppy finish. The label mentions passionfruit and lime. I picked up more of the former than the latter but suspect the colder you drink it the more citrusy the effect. A good beer to accompany Indian, Thai and Mexican cuisine, although it would go equally well with lasagne.

IBS (INVERCARGILL BREWERY SPECIAL)

ALCOHOL
4.7% abv

STYLE
English Special Bitter

 **TOP BREW**

The first beer brewed by the team, this was my favourite. I liked the appearance — tan-brown with a nicely creamy head. There is an enticing aroma of malt and hop suggesting attention has been paid to the balance. The beer is styled on English bitter, and has a sweetish, fruity beginning leading to a nicely hoppy bite at the finish. Best enjoyed at room temperature, IBS is an excellent food beer and I would suggest good, honest pub fare like a Ploughman's lunch with all its bits, which will bring out the individual strengths of the beer.

WASP

ALCOHOL
4.2% abv

STYLE
Golden Ale

This was originally styled as a Kristallweizen and has many of the flavours associated with this international style. You will immediately pick up an underlying fruitiness, with banana and cloves adding interest. For some these may be a little overdominant but I suggest trying it with food before making a final decision. The bite of the beer will complement creamy dishes but I think the better option would be with a spicy curry where the beer's fruitiness will shine.

PITCH BLACK

ALCOHOL
4.5% abv

STYLE
Stout

This beer has the deep brown colour of stout with perhaps a slightly lighter texture than we expect of the style, particularly in the mid-palate. Its texture is soft, its taste full of chocolate and coffee and its finish off-dry. A very drinkable dark beer with plenty of character. My choice of meal match would be a red meat roast, when its gentle bitterness will contribute a welcome balance.

IMPORTED BEERS

THE NEW ZEALAND BEER consumer continues to be well served when it comes to imported beer — perhaps more now than ever. It is possible to purchase almost any beer in the world in this country, if not directly off the shelf then certainly through an indent company or increasingly via the internet.

However, it is very difficult to determine exactly how many foreign beer brands are regularly available. I have developed the list below, which I freely acknowledge is far from exhaustive, by combining the lists of packaged product from a major supermarket chain, a major importer and two highly regarded beer retailers with the beverage lists from a couple of well-known bars that are recognised for the wide range of imported beers they stock.

It should be noted that in recent years improved means of packing and distribution have resulted in imported product arriving here in much better condition. The growing popularity of these beers also means greater turnover and so the product you purchase should be fresher. But this is not always the case and never guaranteed. It is definitely a matter of buyer beware!

The beers below are listed by country of origin. Not all retail outlets stock all the imported beers, and some are available only at restaurants. However, the list does provide a good indication of what is currently being brought into the country.

AUSTRALIA

CARLTON COLD-FILTERED BITTER
ALCOHOL
4.9% abv

Pale straw, full-strength beer with crisp texture, good body-weight and balanced hop bitterness on the palate. There is melon and tropical fruit in the flavour as well. Good balance and lengthy finish.

CARLTON STRIPE
ALCOHOL
4.0% abv

Mid-straw brown with a distinctly hop aroma. The mouth-feel is generous, the texture crisp and clean. The bitterness comes through in the taste, which has some herb and spice notes as well. A pleasantly long aftertaste.

CARLTON CROWN LAGER
ALCOHOL
4.9% abv

Premium golden lager with a crisp, clean mouth-feel and a malty, sweet flavour profile. There is a good dollop of hop flavour but little bitterness. Easy drinking, with a generous refreshing finish.

CASCADE PREMIUM LAGER
ALCOHOL
5.2% abv

A distinctive aroma and a crisp, clean texture that is consistent to the finish. Generous hopping shows on a palate that is full of flavour, including some subtle floral notes.

COOPER'S PREMIUM CLEAR ALE
ALCOHOL
4.9% abv

A yellow-gold colour, a good creamy head and a mild hop aroma introduce this beer, which has a rounded and full-bodied palate of moderate bitterness. There is good mouth-feel and a moderate malt and hop finish.

COOPER'S SPARKLING ALE
ALCOHOL
5.8% abv

Brewed using the top-fermentation method, this Aussie star displays a solid head and distinctive, full-bodied flavour enhanced by a soft, fruity character and sediment that gives a cloudy appearance.

COOPER'S BEST EXTRA STOUT

| ALCOHOL |
| 6.8% abv |

Cooper's Best Extra Stout, also brewed using the top-fermentation method, is a good example of the robust, full-flavoured stout family. The unique, rich, dark texture of the product is produced by specially roasted black malt.

COOPER'S ORIGINAL PALE ALE

| ALCOHOL |
| 4.5% abv |

Fermented in the 'Burton-on-Trent' style, this is made in the same way as Cooper's Sparkling Ale, with a full, fruity flavour. Secondary fermentation produces a fine, cloudy residue in the finished product.

DIAMOND

| ALCOHOL |
| 4.2% abv |

A full-flavoured, golden grain-coloured beer that has fewer calories than regular beer. The aroma is sweet and grassy, while the texture is lightweight and refreshing. Flavourful, with a caramel finish.

FOSTER'S LAGER

| ALCOHOL |
| 4.9% abv |

A light-coloured lager style with a slightly hoppy but yeasty/malty nose. The flavour has full malt character with balanced, clean hop bitterness. Crisp and clean texture, with good mouth-feel and length.

FOSTER'S LIGHT

| ALCOHOL |
| 2.5% abv |

Foster's Light has only half the alcohol content of its famous parent. Its full malt character and clean hop bitterness are combined with a delicate estery, yeasty and malty nose to produce a low-strength beer of excellent length.

FOSTER'S SPECIAL BITTER

| ALCOHOL |
| 2.8% abv |

A refreshing, full-bodied, low-strength beer brewed with extra hops to give a welcome bitter flavour that is consistent from start to finish.

JAMES BOAG'S PREMIUM

| ALCOHOL |
| 5% abv |

Voted Australia's Grand Champion Beer in 1998, this is a European-style lager batch brewed in Tasmania. It is made using pilsner malts, has extra hops added late in production and enjoys an extended maturation period. This combination results in a crisp, pale lager with a delicately yeasty aroma, plenty of flavour and a slight hop dryness on the back palate.

JAMES SQUIRE ALE

ALCOHOL
5% abv

Complex yet easy drinking, and brimming with flavour. There is plenty of deep malt character and some overt hoppiness that results in a long-lasting caramel flavour with a nuttiness to finish.

JAMES SQUIRE PILSENER

ALCOHOL
5% abv

A fine example of the style — crisp and clean with a floral aroma and a dry yeasty taste, with a little citrus zing from the inclusion of Saaz hops, making it refreshing and satisfying.

JAMES SQUIRE PORTER

ALCOHOL
5% abv

This porter has a restrained stout character, showing roasted malt and wheat flavours, with a zippy, dark chocolate taste as well. The hop character is very soft and the texture creamy and light. Plenty of aftertaste encourages a drink-more-of-me attitude.

POWER'S BITTER

ALCOHOL
4.8% abv

This Queensland dark gold lager has a strong hop tang balanced by a sweet palate. There is some bitterness towards the end and it is quite refreshing when chilled.

RESCH'S PILSENER

ALCOHOL
4.6% abv

Traditional pilsner with cut-grass and spice aroma and a smooth palate, followed by a distinct dry, hoppy finish.

RESCH'S REAL

ALCOHOL
4% abv

Unusually hoppy for an Australian beer, this one has an attractive aroma with full-strength bitter taste, a clean texture and sweet malt balance.

SWAN SPECIAL LIGHT

ALCOHOL
0.9% abv

Produced from regular-strength beer using a vacuum distillation process. Almost all of the alcohol is extracted but the character and taste of the beer is kept. It is crisp, clean and distinctly bitter — and it has only half the calories of the average beer.

TOOHEYS BLUE LABEL

ALCOHOL
2.5% abv

Blue Label is made using a high proportion of flavoured crystal malt, mashed at a higher temperature than normal. This ensures good texture and body. Selected hops finish the flavour on a crisp, dry note.

VICTORIA BITTER

ALCOHOL
4.9% abv

Well-balanced fruity/malty and yeasty notes in the aroma. The full malt and increased clean hop bitterness is complemented by a pleasant sweetness on the palate. It has a stronger, drier finish.

Note: In addition, three beers from the Foster's-owned Matilda Bay Brewery have become available since the compiling of this guide: Redback Original (4.7% abv), Beez Neez Wheat Beer (4.7% abv) and Bohemian Pilzner (4.5% abv).

BELGIUM

BELLE VUE KRIEK

ALCOHOL
5.2% abv

Ruby-red with strong cherry aroma and fruity, sweet taste carried by a clean and crisp texture that fills the palate. Very distinctive flavour from start to finish. Some dryness around the sides of the mouth.

BELLE VUE FRAMBOISE

ALCOHOL
5.2% abv

Made from wheat, lambic and raspberries; pink with a strong aroma and fruity, sweet taste; lengthy, pervasive, sweet aftertaste, slightly medicinal.

BELLE VUE GUEUZE

ALCOHOL
5.2% abv

Made from wheat and over-aged hops, showing golden colour. Full-bodied taste with good balance between sweet, bitter and sour influences. Good length.

CHIMAY RED TRAPPIST ALE

ALCOHOL
7% abv

Definite pink blush, a soft, creamy aroma with a good level of hops. Gentle fruit in mouth, with a long, bitter finish. Bottle conditioned.

CHIMAY WHITE TRAPPIST ALE

ALCOHOL
8% abv

Pale peach in colour, this ale has a dry, firm, hoppy aroma. Full of flavour with lots of fruit sweetness on the palate. Will become drier on cellaring.

CHIMAY BLUE TRAPPIST ALE

ALCOHOL
9% abv

Redcurrant fruit and hops aroma; fruity palate; lingering fruit and sherry notes in finish. Very spicy.

DUVEL TOP FERMENTED STRONG BEER

ALCOHOL
8.5% abv

'Doovil' means 'devil' in Flemish. Light fruit and hop aroma; pear-like fruit in mouth; long bittersweet finish with developing hop bitterness towards the finish.

GOUDEN CAROLUS

ALCOHOL
8% abv

This is a Flemish strong brown ale with lovely orange and coriander additions. If it reaches you in good condition you should pick up on some toffee and cedary influences as well, particularly towards the back palate.

HOEGAARDEN WHITE

ALCOHOL
5% abv

Unfiltered, re-fermented and bottle conditioned, this beer has a cloudy appearance. Coriander and Curaçao complement a refreshing sour-sweet taste and a fruity, soft bitter aroma. Moderately smooth and mouth-filling.

HOEGAARDEN GRAND CRU

ALCOHOL
8.7% abv

Hazy, softly golden colour with a subtle, complex flavour and a strong aroma tending toward sweet and delicately hoppy. Creamy texture with plenty of length. Bottle conditioned.

HOEGAARDEN FORBIDDEN FRUIT

ALCOHOL
8.8% abv

Dark red, complex beer brewed with dark malts; well balanced, soft yet dry. Bottle conditioned.

LEFFE BLONDE

ALCOHOL
6.6% abv

A real favourite of mine, this is a strong, flavour-filled beer from Belgium. It is incredibly aromatic and has a delicious bittersweet flavour that is made all the more interesting by its orange and coriander additives. Refreshing and satisfying with a real drink-more-of-me attitude.

LEFFE DARK

ALCOHOL
6.5% abv

Wonderful roasted malts are used in the brewing of this beer, resulting in a deep coffee-brown colour, a fruit and spice Christmas-cake aroma, rich and complex fruit and malt flavours, and a lingering aftertaste. A beer to sip and savour!

LIEFMANS GOUDENBAND

ALCOHOL
8% abv

A classic brown ale from near Oudenaarde in Belgium, this is carefully blended from young and old beer and bottle aged, the result being a toasty beer with a fascinating, slightly sour flavour. Good as an aperitif, to waken the taste buds.

LINDEMANS FRAMBOISE

ALCOHOL
2.5% abv

A raspberry-flavoured lambic beer with a very sweet middle palate and a tartness towards the end. Complex and delicious.

LINDEMANS KRIEK

A true kriek with a real cherry character that pervades both the aroma and the taste. A very good example of the style.

> ALCOHOL
> 4% abv

MARTENS PILS

Another fine import from Belgium, this robust golden lager has good flavour with an easy-drinking malt and hop balance. The texture is fine with a refreshing, spritzy mouth-feel. An excellent beer to enjoy with a meal, particularly over the summer months.

> ALCOHOL
> 4% abv

MORTE SUBITE KRIEK

A well-known and highly regarded cherry-flavoured lambic brew. Nicely balanced with hints of almond in the finish. Delicious and satisfying.

> ALCOHOL
> 4.3%abv

ROCHEFORTE 8

One in a series of Trappist beers, the numeral refers to their gravity in Belgian degrees. This is fruiter than the 6 and not as chocolatey as the 10 and a very pleasant drink.

> ALCOHOL
> 9.2% abv

ROCHEFORTE 10

A strong beer, rich dark-brown in colour with a tonne of malty fruit character with some toffee and chocolate flavours as well. One for gentle supping.

> ALCOHOL
> 11.3% abv

WESTMALLE BRUN DUBBEL

A true abbey beer, this strong tipple has an in-your-face chocolate and malt flavour that envelops the palate and then dries out at the finish. There's every chance you will pick up on some banana character as well.

> ALCOHOL
> 7 % abv

WESTMALLE BLONDE TRIPLE

Another Trappist beer, this time a lighter but even high-strength brew with heaps of fruitiness and a freshness and drinkability deriving from the Saaz hops.

> ALCOHOL
> 9% abv

CANADA

LABATTS BLUE

A fragrant lager with a pleasing golden colour and mellow smoothness that indicates a low bitterness level for very accessible drinking.

ALCOHOL
5% abv

MOOSEHEAD

Clean, crisp sparkling lager with malty undertones, as well as a pleasing sweetness on the palate. The hop influence is subtle but there is a distinct grassiness about the beer that gives it a firm structure and easy-drinking character.

ALCOHOL
5% abv

CHINA

TSING TAO

Tawny-yellow colour; malt nose; malt and hop flavour. Good body, medium-dry malt finish and aftertaste with plenty of hop backing.

ALCOHOL
4.5% abv

ZHUJIANG BEER

Very pale gold with a nutty and grassy aroma. The texture is crisp and clean. An easy-drinking lager style with plenty of hop flavours and some cut-hay character as well.

ALCOHOL
3.8–4.3% abv

CZECH REPUBLIC

BUDEJOVICKY BUDVAR

Gentle hops and toffee-malt aromas; superb balance of malt and hops in the mouth. It has a bittersweet finish with light vanilla hops.

ALCOHOL
5% abv

PILSNER URQUELL

ALCOHOL
4.4% abv

Golden lager with a slight lime hue and a mild, grassy, hop aroma. Full, dry flavour with good length and a hop-bitter finish. A complex, well-made beer.

DENMARK

CARLSBERG GREEN

ALCOHOL
5% abv

A stylish gold-coloured lager with a good body and a vinous character. In the European style, with strong flavour intensity coming from malty fruit flavours. Excellent mouth-feel and generous length.

ELEPHANT BEER

ALCOHOL
7.2% abv

A rich, golden-amber, full-strength beer with some yeasty aromas and an unusually big, fruity palate. At the same time strong, malty flavours are balanced with moderately bitter hops and a slight sweetness. The extra strength of Elephant Beer makes it worthy of respect.

GIRAF GOLD

ALCOHOL
5.6% abv

Richly coloured and smooth-textured, with bittersweet characters on the nose and palate. It has some spice flavours as well. A refreshing aftertaste makes this an interesting food beer.

TUBORG GOLD

ALCOHOL
5.5% abv

This mild pilsner-style beer can be found in beer outlets around the world. It is light straw in colour with a light body and a clean texture. It is moderately full in flavour, but it finishes relatively quickly. The malt and hop influence is there but hardly challenging.

BEER QUOTES 'Beer is the Danish national drink, and the Danish national weakness is another beer.' Clementine Paddleford (1900–67)

FIJI

FIJI BITTER
ALCOHOL
4.6% abv

An ideal beer for the warmer tropical climates. A subtle aroma and a clean texture lead into a sweetish, fruity flavour with just a hint of bitterness. Easy drinking.

FRANCE

KRONENBOURG 1664
ALCOHOL
5% abv

A soft, grainy nose with a subtle, light hoppiness. A light, well-rounded flavour with hop and straw influences. Excellent hop bitterness to finish.

GERMANY

BECKS
ALCOHOL
5% abv

A fresh, malty lager with a hoppy tang. The flavour is rich and complex. The texture is full and the finish long.

BITBURGER PREMIUM
ALCOHOL
4.6% abv

This brew has a pale gold colour. It is light and dry, with a pronounced hop flavour overriding soft maltiness in middle palate; finishes with subtle, elegant bitterness.

DAB
ALCOHOL
4% abv

An easy-drinking pilsner on the light side with some fruitiness and nuttiness n the taste. There is a little hop bitterness at the end just to keep it interesting. Best when chilled and definitely when fresh.

FRANZISKANER

A lovely wheat beer with a caramelly aroma and a grainy texture. It is full flavoured with a touch of allspice or cinnamon towards the end. A great thirst quencher.

ALCOHOL
5% abv

HOLSTEN PREMIUM

Assertive hoppiness and dryness, rounded malty character. Good length.

ALCOHOL
5% abv

JEVER PILSNER

A lovely hoppy lager with a hop-dominant aroma and a yeasty palate, and strong, deliciously dry finish. A crisp, clean texture accentuates the extra dry, hoppy flavour.

ALCOHOL
5.2% abv

KOSTRITZER SCHWARZBIER

Dark-roast malt, chocolate and hop aromas; bitter chocolate in the mouth; big finish packaged with dark fruit chocolate and hops.

ALCOHOL
4.8% abv

LOWENBRAU ORIGINAL

Lively, citric aroma; fine balance of malt and hops in the mouth; a long finish packed with hop bitterness.

ALCOHOL
5.2% abv

RAUNCHENFELSER STEINBIER

This stone-brewed beer is top-fermented with a fine, smoky, caramelised flavour from the immersion of red-hot stones in the brewing vessel.

ALCOHOL
4.9% abv

ROMERKRUG 'STEIN'

Fine champagne-like sparkle, good malt flavour and creamy head. Texture is crisp and clean with good mouth-feel and a sweetish finish.

ALCOHOL
4.9% abv

SCHNEIDER WEISS BEER (HELLE) ORIGINAL

Complex bouquet of banana, cloves and nutmeg, tart fruit in the mouth and creamy, fruity finish with hints of bubble gum.

ALCOHOL
5.4% abv

SCHNEIDER AVENTINUS WEISS DOPPELBOCK

| ALCOHOL |
| 8% abv |

Bronze-red; rich spice and chocolate aroma on palate; more spices, vinous fruit and cloves in the finish. Generous mouth-feel and lengthy finish.

ST PAULI GIRL

| ALCOHOL |
| 5% abv |

A full-flavoured brew, with a wheaty, light and grainy character. Light hop and straw aroma. It shows a clean, fresh palate and a light and crisp texture with a character of style and balance, and it has good length.

WARSTEINER PREMIUM

| ALCOHOL |
| 4.8% abv |

Bright pale gold in colour, with a very hoppy aroma and a complex malt and hop flavour. Excellent balance, big hop finish and a long, dry hop aftertaste.

VELTINS

| ALCOHOL |
| 4.8% abv |

A fresh, easy-drinking pilsner with a cut-grass aroma and a sweetish taste. There is plenty of bitterness to satisfy the hop lover.

INDIA

FLYING HORSE ROYAL LAGER

| ALCOHOL |
| 4% abv |

Pale yellow-gold in colour with a grassy aroma that shows a bit of treacle. This is a crisp and lightweight beer, very mild and sweet with short length and a drier finish.

KALYANI EXPORT SPECIAL

| ALCOHOL |
| 4.8% abv |

Yellow-gold with a lime hue, this beer has no discernible aroma and a lightweight mouth-feel. The texture is clean, the flavour grassy and a little fruity. No length and a crisp finish.

KINGFISHER PREMIUM LAGER

ALCOHOL
5% abv

Yellow-gold with a yellow tint. Hoppy aroma with a bubble-gum note. Crisp and clean, the flavour has malt and hop characters. Lightweight overall and easy drinking.

IRELAND

BEAMISH RED ALE

ALCOHOL
4.5% abv

Distinctive chestnut-red hue and creamy, smooth mouth-feel; distinct hop aroma and exceptional malt/hop balance in the flavour. Full bodied, with full and lengthy aftertaste; best enjoyed well chilled.

BEAMISH IRISH STOUT

ALCOHOL
4.2% abv

Dark, almost black, with a distinct hop aroma. The texture is smooth and refreshing, the flavour rich and mouth-filling with chocolate and roast malt characters. Appealing finish and plenty of length.

MURPHY'S IRISH STOUT

ALCOHOL
4% abv

Smooth, creamy, dark brown stout. A roasted-coffee aroma, medium to heavy body and roasted flavour with chocolate accents; dry finish.

ITALY

PERONI NASTRO AZZURO

ALCOHOL
5.2% abv

A clean and fresh, hoppy nose with some yeasty aroma. A full, crisp palate and residual hop bitterness. Well balanced with good flavour.

> **BEER QUOTES** 'Ale, man, ale's the stuff to drink/For fellows whom it hurts to think.'
> A. E. Housman (1859–1936)

JAPAN

ASAHI SUPER DRY
ALCOHOL
5% abv

This dry Asian beer is one of the best of its type. Asahi invented the dry-brewing process where not all the grain is malted. Distinctive; crisp and light; light hop flavour; best served cold.

KIRIN
ALCOHOL
4.5% abv

Highly aromatic and highly flavoured (leathery, flavour of wet paper), plenty of length. Kirin is a fully hopped beer with loads of taste. It is a lager of substance, clean and well balanced.

SAPPORO PREMIUM LAGER
ALCOHOL
5% abv

Grainy aroma; malty in the mouth; dry finish with some hop notes.

KOREA

HITE BEER
ALCOHOL
4.5% abv

Hazy, pale gold; light malt and hop nose; light, dry, faint hop flavour; a little sweetness in the finish. Light body with slight dry-malt aftertaste.

MEXICO

CORONA EXTRA
ALCOHOL
4.6% abv

A hoppy nose with a tinge of cornmeal and a slightly yeasty, maize character. Texture is crisp and dry, with a powerful initial taste of sweet malt and hop. This is a simple and refreshing beer with a light gold colour and fruity palate.

SOL

A popular summer beer, light straw in colour with negligible aroma. The texture is lightweight and fizzy. Flavour is dry with cornmeal characteristics. Unusual and quite enjoyable.

ALCOHOL
4.1% abv

NAMIBIA

TAFEL LAGER

Pale straw-gold in colour with a floral/perfumed aroma. The texture is creamy with good mouth-feel and medium body. The flavour has hints of tropical fruit over the top of the malt sweetness. There is some hop bitterness towards the end that provides a crisp finish.

ALCOHOL
4% abv

WINDHOEK LAGER

Straw-gold, with both malt and hop in the aroma. Texture is crisp and clean with generous mouth-feel. The flavour is malty sweet with some dryness on the sides of the palate suggesting hop. It's light, mildly bitter and refreshing at the end.

ALCOHOL
4% abv

WINDHOEK LIGHT

Pale gold with mild aroma and flavour. On the nose slightly grainy and musty. Texture is lightweight and crisp. Some malt sweetness; melon and citrus notes as well. Short finish leaving clean aftertaste.

ALCOHOL
2% abv

THE NETHERLANDS

GROLSCH

Internationally recognised for its unique 473-millilitre swing-top bottle with the porcelain stopper, Grolsch is now available in more

ALCOHOL
5% abv

conventional packaging. It is a pale lager with a light, well-rounded crisp body, a hint of malt sweetness and a lingering finish.

ORANJEBOOM PREMIUM LAGER

ALCOHOL
5% abv

An elegant golden-coloured beer from Rotterdam. It has plenty of interesting, malty flavour together with a mild bitterness towards the end. It is in the lager or pilsner style and is therefore best served with chicken or shellfish without too many competing flavours.

PIRATE

ALCOHOL
8.5% abv

An extra-strong malty beer, well-balanced and with a lingering aftertaste. Serve it up with steak and kidney pie.

ALFA EDEL PILS

ALCOHOL
5% abv

Light gold with the aroma of sweet, old rose petals. Texture is light and airy, and sweet malt character makes an easy-drinking lager.

AMSTERDAM

ALCOHOL
4% abv

Another easy-drinking lager with acceptable malt and hop balance. With no overt aroma and a lightweight texture this beer is best enjoyed ice-cold.

3 HORSES

ALCOHOL
4.3% abv

Made at the Three Horseshoe Brewery in Breda, founded in 1538, an uncomplicated lager with mild to soft texture and low bitterness.

THE PHILIPPINES

SAN MIGUEL

ALCOHOL
5% abv

An interesting golden lager, at 5% abv it's on the strong side but it is a refreshing, tasty brew — a little sweet, a little dry, with a lingering spicy aftertaste.

SAMOA

VAILIMA

Brewed to a German recipe, this is a standard golden lager with some European influence. Sweetish, fruity, easy drinking.

ALCOHOL
4.9% abv

SINGAPORE

ABC STOUT

Opaque, brown head; off-dry malt and hop nose. Palate is complex; herbal roasted-malt flavour until the finish that is dry and faintly burnt. Long, off-dry, malt aftertaste with some liquorice and molasses.

ALCOHOL
8% abv

ANCHOR PILSENER BEER

A deep gold in colour, this beer offers a hop and malt nose; slightly roasted-malt flavour; malt hop finish; decent balance with good body; long malt and hop aftertaste.

ALCOHOL
5% abv

RAFFLES LAGER

A light straw-coloured, tropical brew with a fruity aroma and a full, smooth mouth-feel. A moderately sweet flavour and some dryness on the back palate. Good length.

ALCOHOL
4.5% abv

TIGER

Pale yellow-gold with a mild aroma and slightly syrupy texture. The flavour is mild and clean with high sweetness and a trace of hop bitterness.

ALCOHOL
5% abv

SOUTH AFRICA

BAVARIA 'EDEL' LAGER

| ALCOHOL |
| 5% abv |

Lime-gold in colour with a good head, it has no discernible aroma. The texture is crisp and dry and fairly complex. The flavour is full with grassy/grainy characters and a nice hop/malt balance. There is a good finish with plenty of aftertaste.

CASTLE LAGER

| ALCOHOL |
| 5% abv |

Very pale gold in colour with a moderately hoppy aroma with some straw influences as well. The texture is crisp and clean with good mouth-weight. On the palate it is refreshingly hoppy with a hop bitterness balanced by some fruity sweetness on the finish. Good drinking.

KALTENBERG 'ROYAL' LAGER

| ALCOHOL |
| 5% abv |

Pale yellow-gold with a malty, sweet-fruit aroma. Smooth with lots of body; flavour has molasses and treacly influences and a good hop balance. There is plenty of length, a bittersweet finish and an off-dry aftertaste. A classy lager.

THAILAND

SINGHA

| ALCOHOL |
| 5.9% abv |

Mid-straw in colour with a moderate aroma of malt and hops. The texture is rich and quite weighty, and somewhat oily. The flavour is mild with bittersweet influences. There is reasonable length with a sweetish finish.

BEER QUOTES 'Would I were in an alehouse in London. I would give all my fame for a pot of ale, and safety.' William Shakespeare (1564–1616)

TURKEY

EFES PILSENER PREMIUM

The Premium gets its pale yellow-gold colour and texture from the bright Pils malt used in its production. It has a musty, grainy aroma and a peppery and spicy flavour with average length and a reasonably hoppy finish.

ALCOHOL
5% abv

EFES PILSENER LIGHT

This is a pale straw colour with a subtle aroma and a refreshing texture. It is crisp with a soft, malty palate at the front, which fades to some dryness on the short finish.

ALCOHOL
2.7% abv

EFES PILSENER EXTRA

Brewed with 'extra' malt and hops, this beer has a rich and fruity aroma. Creamy texture and full flavour carried through the entire palate to the finish by a generous alcohol level. Worthy of respect.

ALCOHOL
7% abv

EFES PILSENER DARK

A classic dark beer, deep brown in colour with a gentle chocolate/caramel aroma. The flavour combines good malt character with a soft hop finish. The smooth texture and generous mouth-feel make this a very drinkable beer.

ALCOHOL
5% abv

UNITED KINGDOM

1698 CELEBRATION ALE

Made with only Kentish hops, this beer is a golden honey colour with good mouth-feel and well-balanced fruit, hop and malt flavours. Plenty of length and a sweet dry finish.

ALCOHOL
6.5% abv

ABBOT ALE

Rich, strong and robust with a distinct malt fruit and toffee flavour. Plenty of body and a lingering, slightly bittersweet finish.

ALCOHOL
5% abv

BADGER COUNTRY BITTER

Mid-gold in colour with a mild malt aroma. Good mouth-feel and full flavour of malt and green grass. Some herb and spice characters. Traditional bitter finish.

ALCOHOL
4% abv

BASS PALE ALE

A deep, rich, amber, traditionally brewed British pale ale with a full body and pleasant bitterness.

ALCOHOL
5% abv

BELHAVEN ST ANDREW'S ALE

Rich and peppery hop aroma with fruit notes, full malt and nut flavour with good hop character. Balanced with an intense, dry after-palate.

ALCOHOL
4.6% abv

BELHAVEN SCOTTISH ALE

This is a lovely session beer with lots of body and flavour to match. It looks great in the glass.

ALCOHOL
3.9% abv

BELHAVEN WEE HEAVY

Best kept for winter months, this beer is rich and flavoursome with a touch of almond, plenty of malt fruit and a creamy texture. Not as strong as some in the style but a heady brew nonetheless.

ALCOHOL
6.5% abv

BISHOP'S FINGER STRONG ALE

Golden brown with a slight red hue, Bishop's Finger is full bodied with a creamy texture. Rich fruit and malt flavours dominate, providing a long finish and a sweet-toffee aftertaste.

ALCOHOL
5.4% abv

BODDINGTON'S PUB ALE

ALCOHOL
4.8% abv

A classic British draught ale famous for its thick, creamy head. Boddington's has a full-bodied, malty flavour that lingers through to a creamy, smooth finish.

BURTON'S CREAMY ALE

ALCOHOL
4.2% abv

Very dark brown in colour, Burton's Creamy Ale is a visual delight — a mass of tiny bubbles disappears to produce a glass of crystal-clear, nut-brown beer capped by about 20 millimetres of creamy head. A chocolate/coffee flavour, full and rich, and a lengthy, semi-bitter finish.

CAFFREY'S IRISH ALE

ALCOHOL
4.8% abv

Caffrey's was inspired by Thomas Caffrey, founder of the famous Mountain Brewery in Ireland. A creamy texture settles tantalisingly slowly, to give a superb, smooth mouth-feel. A malty, sweet flavour with a gentle, hoppy finish.

CHARLES WELL'S BOMBARDIER BITTER

ALCOHOL
5.5% abv

A deliciously bitter ale, with oodles of fruit and malt. It's big and robust with just a hint of roasted malt and a clean dry finish.

DOUBLE DIAMOND BURTON ALE

ALCOHOL
5% abv

Brewed from pale chocolate malts. Good hop palate and refreshing pale ale style. In-can nitrogenised Draughtflow system.

FULLER'S LONDON PRIDE

ALCOHOL
4.7% abv

A copper-coloured ale with an assertive, malty flavour, balancing hop bitterness and a lingering fruit/hoppy flavour. Marvellous complexity with a high degree of fruitiness, hops and malt, with only medium bitterness. A hint of caramel is balanced nicely by the hop, which is noticeable only after it has warmed in your glass for a while. The finish is equally complex, with a smooth, lingering mellowness that's neither sweet nor dry — just memorable.

JOHN SMITH'S BITTER

ALCOHOL
3.8% abv

Best drunk through its rich, creamy head, this beer is dark brown-amber in colour. It is creamy and full bodied with a distinctive, sharp, hop flavour and bitterness balanced by chocolate malts. Silky-smooth to the finish.

KING & BARNES FESTIVE

ALCOHOL
5.3% abv

A bottle-conditioned beer, very hoppy with a herbal aroma and a big, smooth fruitiness.

MCEWAN'S EXPORT PALE ALE

ALCOHOL
4.5% abv

A provocative beer with a distinctive and unusual flavour. Smooth and crisp, it is moderately sweet with at the same time an interesting dryness that catches the back palate. Real character.

MCEWAN'S SCOTCH ALE

ALCOHOL
8% abv

A very strong and rich winter warmer in the classic style. Deep brown-red in colour with a dark chocolate aroma and a full body. Smooth and full of malty flavours, with a slight, cleansing, hop finish.

MCEWAN'S LAGER

ALCOHOL
4.1% abv

Rich golden-grain colour with a hop aroma; crisp and clean texture; both malt and hop influence the flavour; a balanced, satisfying finish.

MCEWAN'S EXPORT IPA

ALCOHOL
4.5% abv

Best served well chilled, this beer is the colour of dry hay. It has a mild aroma of grass and grain and a smooth, crisp texture and mouthfeel. There is definite malt in the flavour as well as a distinct roast-barley note. A refreshing, slightly bitter finish.

MARSTON'S OWD ROGER

ALCOHOL
7.6% abv

A strong old ale, this warms the very cockles of the palate as well as the heart. You will pick up touches of liquorice and caramel and there is even some fortified wine/port-like character in the finish.

MARSTON'S OYSTER STOUT

ALCOHOL
4.5% abv

This is a lovely dry stout just right for supping in front of the fire with a bucket of freshly shucked Bluff oysters. If you can't get Bluff oysters, settle for any kind of oyster just to experience the match with this beer.

MASTER BREW

ALCOHOL
4% abv

A rich tan-brown, traditional ale with creamy texture, medium bitterness and a fuller flavour of mellow malt and caramel.

NEWCASTLE BROWN ALE

ALCOHOL
4.7% abv

An interesting and complex beer, clean and light, with a slightly roasted aroma and a smoky, nostalgic character and rich flavour. Good, simple, brown-ale style that will make a good session beer.

OLD SPECKLED HEN

ALCOHOL
5.2% abv

Morland's Old Speckled Hen has a superb, rich, malty, estery aroma and a wonderful, mouth-filling, warming flavour bursting with body. Malt and toffee flavours combine with bitterness on the back of the tongue to give a balanced sweetness that is not cloying.

ORIGINAL PORTER ALE

ALCOHOL
5% abv

Deep chocolate-brown in colour, with a malty fruit, Christmas-cake aroma; creamy mouth-filling body; full, rich chocolate and liquorice flavours. This is a meal of a beer, with character and a lengthy, satisfying, bitter-sweet finish.

SAMUEL SMITH'S NUT BROWN ALE

ALCOHOL
5% abv

Malty and bitter, this beer is full of texture with a nutty finish to the palate.

SAMUEL SMITH'S OLD PALE ALE

ALCOHOL
5% abv

Generous aroma of hops with a smooth texture and a malty flavour. Good length.

SAMUEL SMITH'S TADDY PORTER

ALCOHOL
5% abv

Similar to a dry stout but lighter in body. Quite fruity on the aroma and in flavour.

SAMUEL SMITH'S IMPERIAL STOUT

ALCOHOL
5% abv

Deep chocolate-brown in colour, with a rich, malt aroma with traces of toffee. Good mouth-feel and a rich, complex finish.

SKOL SPECIAL

ALCOHOL
9% abv

A very strong lager with a smooth texture and a challenging aftertaste that will delight hop lovers.

SPITFIRE BITTER ALE

ALCOHOL
5.5% abv

Mid-straw in colour, with a dominating hop aroma, Spitfire has a crisp, dry texture and lightweight mouth-feel. The hops come through again on the palate, with some cut-grass and some hay influence providing both hop bitterness and a lingering, dry aftertaste.

TANGLEFOOT

ALCOHOL
5% abv

Very pale straw colour with an equally light texture and moderate mouth-feel. Good balance of flavours showing generous hop. Dry rather than bitter.

TENNENT'S LAGER

ALCOHOL
5% abv

Yellow-gold in colour, Tennent's Lager has a mild straw-like aroma with some yeastiness. It is full bodied but clean and crisp, and the flavour has malty accents and is somewhat fruity with mild hop influence.

TENNENT'S SUPER LAGER

ALCOHOL
9% abv

One of the strongest lagers brewed in the UK, Tennent's Super is light gold in colour and appreciably strong in taste, with lengthy hop flavour and bitterness balanced by some welcome malt character. A small glass of this weighty brew makes a fine digestive.

TETLEY EXPORT BITTER

ALCOHOL
5% abv

Full-strength bitter beer. Rich, creamy flavour; good malt and hops balance; dry finish; in-can nitrogenised Draughtflow system.

THEAKSTON'S OLD PECULIAR

ALCOHOL
6% abv

A strong Yorkshire ale with deep dark-brown colour and rich body. Moderately sweetish and well-rounded with a fresh, lighter-than-expected flavour that has smoky, meaty-bacon influences. Smooth and satisfying with a long, rich, concentrated palate.

THEAKSTON'S BEST BITTER

ALCOHOL
3.8% abv

Another to drink through its head. A creamy, full-bodied texture with a clean edge to it. The flavour is full with malt and a touch of yeast character. Very mouth-filling, with a generous finish.

YOUNG'S LUXURY DOUBLE CHOCOLATE STOUT

ALCOHOL
5% abv

From every angle this beer screams chocolate. Its rich deep mahogany colour, velvety soft texture and incredibly complex bittersweet flavour all clearly and unreservedly announce chocolate, chocolate, chocolate. But this is no sickly-sweet cocoa concoction. The bit of the hop and the 5% alcohol confirm its credentials as a bona fide dark beer.

YOUNG'S OLD NICK

ALCOHOL
7.2% abv

Dark beer made in the traditional barley wine style with a rich malt character and a winey taste. One to sup and savour.

YOUNG'S OATMEAL STOUT

ALCOHOL
5% abv

A well-made brew with a velvety texture, a fruity aroma and a wheaty, biscuity flavour. Very drinkable.

YOUNG'S RAM ROD

ALCOHOL
5% abv

The addition of Kent Goldings hops sets this beer apart from others and encourages the development of a fruit and hop balance that is very refreshing.

YOUNG'S SPECIAL LONDON ALE

ALCOHOL
6.4% abv

Bottle conditioned with only a touch of yeast, this is a beautifully crafted beer and a real pleasure to drink. Plenty of all the essential ingredients in complete harmony, including the hop bitterness that punctuates the finish.

UNITED STATES

BAD FROG ORIGINAL

ALCOHOL
4.5% abv

A golden amber beer with a smooth but distinct rich malt character resulting from the long cold-maturation time. Moderate length.

BAD FROG LEMON LAGER

ALCOHOL
3.25% abv

Extremely light and smooth beer with a refreshing hint of lemon. A favourite with lager and lime fans.

BLACKENED VOODOO LAGER

ALCOHOL
4.95% abv

Deep amber-rose in colour, with a pleasant malt and hop aroma. Big, dry-toasted malt flavour with some hops in the back and a dry hop aftertaste. This is an all-malt beer made from five different malts and Mt Hood and Cascade hops.

BUDWEISER

ALCOHOL
5% abv

Another lightweight, light straw-coloured beer, with a sweet aroma and very little mouth-feel. Mild honey and tropical fruit flavour, uncomplicated by hop influences. No finish to speak of.

DIXIE LAGER

ALCOHOL
4.5% abv

Gold, with a touch of amber, lightly hopped with a slightly sour malt aroma. Light body, refreshing hop flavour, medium-dry finish and aftertaste.

LONE STAR

ALCOHOL
4.6% abv

Gold, with a light malt and hop aroma. Flavour to match its light body and a medium-dry finish with little aftertaste.

MILLER GENUINE DRAFT

ALCOHOL
4.7% abv

The top-selling US beer in New Zealand. Straw-gold in colour, it has a malty aroma with floral tones and plenty of sweetness in the flavour. A light, refreshing quaffer.

ROLLING ROCK

ALCOHOL
5% abv

Easy-drinking lager with a freshly cut grass aroma, a light body and a very lightly hopped finish.

REFERENCES

Aidells, B. and Kelly, D., *Real Beer and Good Eats*, Knopf, New York, 1995

Gordon, D., *Speight's: The Story of Dunedin's Historic Brewery*, Avon, Dunedin, 1993

Jackson, M., *Beer*, Penguin, London, 1998

Jackson, M., *Beer Companion*, Running Press, Philadelphia, 1994

Jackson, M., *The New World Guide to Beer*, Running Press, Philadelphia, 1988

Jackson, M., *Michael Jackson's Pocket Beer Book*, Mitchell Beazley, London, 2000, 2001

La France, P., *Cooking and Eating with Beer*, John Wiley & Sons, New York, 1997

McLauchlan, G., *The Story of Beer*, Viking, Auckland, 1994

Saunders, L., *Cooking with Beer*, Time Life Books, Virginia, 1996

There are many excellent beer and brewing sites on the internet. Amongst the best are www.beermasters.com and www.realbeer.com. Another site of interest to New Zealanders is www.realbeer.co.nz.

Sparging: The New Zealand Brewers News is available at www.realbeer.co.nz.

GLOSSARY

THIS GLOSSARY WAS COMPILED in the main using definitions supplied by the American Beer Masters Tasting Society. The profiles applied to particular beer styles (bock, pilsner, stout, etc.) are very general. There are commonly many variations of each style, which highlight differences between countries, brewing preferences and ingredients.

ABV amount of alcohol in beer in terms of percentage volume of alcohol per volume of beer

ACIDIC (see sour)

ADJUNCT fermentable material used as a substitute for traditional grains to make beer lighter bodied or cheaper. Adjuncts such as fruit can also be used to alter flavour.

ALCOHOLIC warming taste of ethanol and higher alcohol

ALE beer distinguished by use of top-fermenting yeast. Top-fermenting yeasts perform at warmer temperatures than yeasts used to brew lager beer and their by-products are more evident in taste and aroma. Fruitiness and esters are often part of ale's character.

ALT German word for old

ALTBIER style of beer from the Dusseldorf district of Germany made using top-fermenting yeasts and cold-conditioned. Usually copper in colour, mashed only from barley malt, 4.5–4.7% abv.

AMBER a colour between pale and dark brown, with a hint of red

AROMA HOPS varieties of hop chosen to impart bouquet

ASTRINGENT drying, puckering taste; tannic. Derives from boiling the grains, long mashes, over-sparging or sparging with hard water.

BARLEY a cereal grain that is malted for use in the grist that becomes the mash in the brewing of beer

BEER fermented beverage made from grain, water, hops, yeast and sometimes adjuncts

BITTER English term for well-hopped ale, most commonly presented in draught form

BITTERNESS the perception of a bitter flavour in beer, derived from hops or malt husks; a sensation on the back of the tongue

BLACK MALT partially malted barley roasted at high temperatures; black malt gives a dark colour and roasted flavour to beer

BOCK German term for strong beer. Commonly distinguished by copper to dark brown colour; full body; malty sweet character dominating the aroma and flavour with a hint of chocolate; low bitterness; low hop flavour; no hop aroma; no fruitiness or esters; low to medium diacetyl is okay.

BODY thickness and mouth-filling property of a beer

BOTTLE CONDITIONING secondary fermentation and maturation in the bottle, creating complex aromas and flavours

BREW-PUB a pub that makes beer and sells at least half of it on the premises. Known in the United Kingdom as a home-brew house and in Germany as a house brewery.

BREWHOUSE equipment used to make beer

BUTTERSCOTCH (see diacetyl)

CAMRA an organisation in England founded in the mid-1960s to preserve the production of cask-conditioned beers and ales

CARAMEL a cooked sugar that is used to add colour and alcohol content to beer, often used in place of more expensive malted barley

CARAMEL MALT a sweet, copper-coloured malt imparting both colour and flavour to beer. It has a high concentration of unfermentable sugars that sweetens the beer and contributes to head retention.

CARBONATION sparkle caused by carbon dioxide, either created during fermentation or injected later

CASK a closed barrel-shaped container for beer, available in various sizes and now usually made of metal. The bung in a cask of 'real' beer or ale must be made of wood to allow the pressure to be relieved, as the fermentation of the beer in the cask continues.

CASK CONDITIONING secondary fermentation and maturation in the cask at the point of sale. It creates light carbonation.

CERAVISAPHILE enthusiast, lover or fan of beer, taken from the Latin word for beer, *cerevisia*

CHILL-HAZE cloudiness caused by precipitation of protein-tannin compound at low temperatures; does not affect flavour

CLOVE-LIKE spicy character reminiscent of cloves, present in some wheat beers; if excessive it may derive from wild yeast

CONDITIONING period of maturation intended to impart 'condition' (natural carbonation). Warm conditioning further develops the complex of flavours; cold conditioning imparts a clean, round taste.

CONTRACT BEER beer made by one brewery and then marketed by a company calling itself a brewery; the latter uses the brewing facilities of the former

DARK BEER an imprecise term for many unrelated styles of dark coloured brews

DIACETYL a volatile compound in beer that contributes to a butterscotch flavour, measured in parts per million

DRY-HOPPING the addition of dry hops to fermenting or ageing beer to increase its hop character or aroma

ESTER a volatile flavour compound, often fruity, flowery or spicy, naturally created in fermentation

EXPORT a word historically applied to any beer of superior quality suitable for export to a foreign country. It implied a high level of quality. Closely associated with Dortmunder-style lager.

FERMENTATION the conversion of sugars into ethyl alcohol and carbon dioxide through the action of yeast

FRUITY flavour and aroma of bananas, strawberries, apples or other fruit; caused by high-temperature fermentation and certain yeast strains

GRAINY tasting like cereal or raw grain

GREEN BEER beer that has fermented but not completed the ageing process

HAND PUMP a device for dispensing draught beer operated by hand. The use of a hand pump allows cask-conditioned beer to be served without the use of pressurised carbon dioxide.

HEFE a German word meaning 'yeast', used mostly in conjunction with wheat (weiss)

beers to denote that the beer is bottled or kegged with the yeast in suspension (hefe-weiss). These beers are cloudy, frothy and very refreshing.

HOPS herb added to boiling wort or fermenting beer to impart a bitter aroma and flavour

INDIA PALE ALE pale to deep amber or copper colour; medium body; medium maltiness; high hop bitterness; medium to high hop flavour and aroma; fruity, estery character; alcohol strength evident; low diacetyl is okay

KRIEK Belgian lambic beer that has been fermented with ripe cherries in the primary fermentation

LACE foamy residue of a beer's head that clings to the inside of the glass as the beer is consumed. Many experts consider the 'Belgian lace' a sign of well-made beer.

LAGER beer made with bottom-fermenting yeast strains at colder fermentation temperatures than an ale. The cooler environment inhibits the natural production of esters and other by-products, creating a crisper-tasting product.

LAMBIC-STYLE ALE a Belgian style of ale that has gone through spontaneous fermentation; intensely and cleanly sour; no hop bitterness, flavour or aroma; fruity, estery character; uniquely aromatic; effervescent. Malted barley and unmalted wheat and stale, old hops are used. Cloudiness is acceptable.

LIGHT-STRUCK a skunk-like smell resulting from exposure to light

LIQUOR water used in the brewing process, included in the mash or used to sparge the grains

MAINSTREAM mass-produced beer enjoyed by many New Zealanders. Generally it is malt, sweetish, only lightly hopped with a moderately firm body, little aftertaste and no great palate-challenging characteristics. Line a few mainstream beers up and most drinkers would find it difficult to spot identify 'their' brand.

MALT the grain, usually barley, used as the foundation ingredient of beer

MALTING the process by which barley is steeped in water, germinated then kilned to convert insoluble starch to soluble substances and sugar

MEDICINAL chemical or phenolic character; can be the result of wild yeast, or contact with plastic or sanitiser residue

METALLIC tasting tinny, blood-like or coin-like; may come from bottle caps

MOUTH-FEEL a sensation derived from the consistency or viscosity of a beer

MUSTY mouldy, mildew character; can be the result of cork or bacterial infection

OXIDISED stale flavour of wet cardboard, paper, rotten pineapple or sherry, as a result of oxygen affecting the beer as it ages or is exposed to high temperatures

PASTEURISATION the heating of beer to 60–79°C to stabilise it microbiologically. Flash-pasteurisation is applied very briefly, for 15–60 seconds, by heating the beer as it passes through the pipe. Alternatively, bottled beer can be passed on a conveyor belt through a heated tunnel; this more gradual process takes at least 20 minutes and sometimes much longer.

PET North Island term for a 2-litre plastic container commonly used by customers to collect beer from a brewery. Known in the South Island as a rigger.

PILSENER (PILSNER, PILS) colour is pale to golden; light to medium body; high hop bitterness; medium hop flavour and aroma; low maltiness in aroma and flavour; no fruitiness or esters; very low diacetyl is okay

PORTER black colour; no roasted barley character; sharp bitterness of black malt without much burnt or charcoal flavour; medium to full body; malty sweetness; medium to high hop bitterness; up to medium hop flavour and aroma; fruity, estery character and low diacetyl okay

QUAFF to drink in large draughts or to drink deeply. In Australia and New Zealand a quaffer is typically a lightweight, unchallenging beer with no special character that is consumed in large quantities as a thirst quencher.

RIGGER South Island term for a 2-litre plastic or glass container, in the North Island called a PET and sometimes a flagon

SAISON seasonal summer beer from the French-speaking districts of Belgium. These are top-fermenting brews with a citric character that refreshes the palate. Typically 5.5–8% abv.

SALTY flavour like table salt, experienced on the side of the tongue

SECONDARY FERMENTATION stage of fermentation occurring in a closed container, lasting from several weeks to several months

SHELF LIFE the length of time a beer will retain its peak drinkability. The shelf life for commercially produced beers is usually a maximum of four months.

SOUR/ACIDIC vinegary or lemony; caused by bacterial infection

SPARGE to spray grist with hot water in order to remove soluble sugars (maltose); this takes place at the end of the mash

STOUT black, opaque colour; light to medium body; medium to high hop bitterness; roasted barley character; sweet maltiness and caramel malt evident; no hop flavour or aroma; some acidity/sourness okay; low to medium alcohol; low to medium diacetyl

SULPHUR-LIKE reminiscent of rotten eggs or burnt matches; a by-product of some yeasts

SWEET tasting like sugar; experienced on the front of the tongue

TARTNESS taste caused by acidic flavours

TRAPPIST top-fermented, bottled-conditioned beers brewed by Trappist monks. There are only six true Trappist breweries still in operation (five in Belgium, one in the Netherlands): Chimay, Orval, Rochefort, Westmalle, Sint Sixtus and Schaapskooi. Only a beer made at one of these breweries can use the term Trappist.

VINOUS reminiscent of wine

WEISSBIER German term for white beer indicating the pale colour of a beer made from wheat

WEIZENBIER German for wheat beer

WINY sherry-like flavour caused by warm fermentation or oxidation in very old beer

WITBIER Dutch/Flemish term for white beer made from wheat

X, XX, XXX, XXXX marks placed on casks by monastery brewers. The higher number of Xs, the greater the quality of the brew.

YEASTY yeast-like flavour; a result of yeast in suspension or beer sitting too long on sediment

INDEX

NOTE: **BREWERY, RESTAURANT AND** bar names are in **bold** type; brewers' and owners' names are in *italic* type. Page numbers in *italic* indicate illustrations of labels.